The African & Middle Eastern World 600–1500

Teaching Guide

UNIVERSITY PRESS

Oxford University Press, Inc., publishes works that further
Oxford University's objective of excellence
in research, scholarship, and education.

Oxford   New York
Auckland   Cape Town   Dar es Salaam   Hong Kong   Karachi
Kuala Lumpur   Madrid   Melbourne   Mexico City   Nairobi
New Delhi   Shanghai   Taipei   Toronto

With offices in
Argentina   Austria   Brazil   Chile   Czech Republic   France   Greece
Guatemala   Hungary   Italy   Japan   Poland   Portugal   Singapore
South Korea   Switzerland   Thailand   Turkey   Ukraine   Vietnam

Copyright © 2005 by Oxford University Press, Inc.

Published by Oxford University Press, Inc.
198 Madison Avenue, New York, NY, 10016
www.oup.com

Oxford is a registered trademark of Oxford University Press

All rights reserved. No part of this publication may be reproduced,
stored in a retrieval system, or transmitted, in any form or by any means,
electronic, mechanical, photocopying, recording, or otherwise,
without the prior permission of Oxford University Press.

ISBN-13: 978-0-19-522254-8 (California edition)   ISBN-13: 978-0-19-522345-3

Writer: Erin Cleary
Project Director: Jacqueline A. Ball
Education Consultant: Diane L Brooks, Ed.D.
Editors: Georgia Scurletis, Katherine Schulten
Design: dlabnyc

Casper Grathwohl, Publisher

Printed in the United States of America
on acid-free paper

THE AFRICAN & MIDDLE EASTERN WORLD, 600–1500 FILMS AND DOCUMENTARIES

Consider using the following films, videos, and DVDs to stimulate student interest in the subject or for extension and enrichment. Teachers should preview all films and be aware that, like historical fiction, films are not always accurate in details.

Arabia: Sand, Sea, & Sky (1991). From the National Geographic Society. This tour of Arabia's natural world, from the Red Sea to the mountains to the desert, is available on VHS.

Byzantium, The Lost Empire (1997). From Discovery Home Video. This video examines the history of Byzantium, the first Christian empire and the last legacy of ancient Greece and Rome before it fell to the Ottoman Turks. Filmed on location in nine countries, the film includes footage of the gates of Constantinople, Hagia Sophia, and St. Mark's in Venice.

The Elephants of Timbuktu (1994). From A&E Home Video. In this film, available on VHS, a herd of wild elephants lives in close proximity to a tribe known as the Tuaregs in a remote West African desert.

The Hajj (1997). From MPI Home Video. Originally broadcast on the television program *Nightline* in April 1997, this footage is available on VHS. It documents the hajj, the holy pilgrimage to Mecca made by Muslims during the last month of the Islamic year.

Inside Islam. From History Channel Video. Traces the roots of Islam back to the Hebrew Bible and discusses how the Five Pillars, the religion's central tenets, helped spread Islam to the far corners of the world. This film includes interviews from contemporary experts who speak about what the Quran says about war, violence, and suicide, and how these words have been co-opted by extremists.

Lost City of Arabia (1996). From PBS Home Video. Explores the Rub al Khali desert of southern Arabia, where it is said that a fabulous city called Ubar once thrived, only to be swallowed up by the dunes. This show also has a companion website: *www.pbs.org/wgbh/nova/ubar/*.

The Message (1976). Directed by Moustapha Akkad, this is an epic drama about the story of Islam.

Muhammad: Legacy of a Prophet (2002). A documentary about the prophet Muhammad, directed by Omar Al-Qattan.

Wonders of the African World (1999). From PBS Home Video. This documentary takes the viewer on a journey through the African continent to the lost wonders of the African world, including the Black kingdoms of the Nile, the Swahili coast, Slave kingdoms, the Road to Timbuktu, and the lost cities of the South.

CONTENTS

Note to the Teacher — 5

The Medieval & Early Modern World Program — 6
  Using the Teaching Guide and Student Study Guide

Improving Literacy with *The Medieval & Early Modern World* — 16

Group Projects — 20

Teaching Strategies for *The African & Middle Eastern World, 600–1500*
  Chapter 1   Camels, Caravans, and the Ka'ba: The Arabian Peninsula around 600 — 26
  Chapter 2   The Messenger of Allah: Muhammad and the Beginning of Islam — 32
  Chapter 3   The Sword of Allah: The Islamic Expansion — 38
  Chapter 4   Managing the Empire: Islam Grows into an Empire of Faith — 44
  Chapter 5   The House of Islam: The First Worldwide Civilization — 50
  Chapter 6   Living by the Rules: Ulama and Philosophers — 56
  Chapter 7   House of Wisdom: Islamic Arts and Sciences — 62
  Chapter 8   Now It's Istanbul, Not Constantinople: The Ottoman Empire — 68
  Chapter 9   Where Gold Grows as Carrots Do: Ghana and the African Grasslands — 74
  Chapter 10 Saddlebags Stuffed with Gold: The Empires of Mali and Songhay — 80
  Chapter 11 Onis and Obas: The Forest Kings of West Africa — 86
  Chapter 12 There's Treasure in Those Hills!: — 92
              Great Zimbabwe and the Shona of Southern Africa
  Chapter 13 The Emperor's Giraffe: East Africa's Swahili Coast — 98

Wrap-Up Test — 104

Rubrics — 106

Graphic Organizers — 110

Answer Key (Teaching Guide and Student Study Guide) — 118

HISTORY FROM OXFORD UNIVERSITY PRESS

"A thoroughly researched political and cultural history... makes for a solid resource for any collection."
– *School Library Journal*

THE WORLD IN ANCIENT TIMES
RONALD MELLOR AND AMANDA H. PODANY, EDS.
THE EARLY HUMAN WORLD
THE ANCIENT NEAR EASTERN WORLD
THE ANCIENT EGYPTIAN WORLD
THE ANCIENT SOUTH ASIAN WORLD
THE ANCIENT CHINESE WORLD
THE ANCIENT GREEK WORLD
THE ANCIENT ROMAN WORLD
THE ANCIENT AMERICAN WORLD

"Bringing history out of the Dark Ages!"

THE MEDIEVAL AND EARLY MODERN WORLD
BONNIE G. SMITH, ED.
THE EUROPEAN WORLD, 400-1450
THE AFRICAN AND MIDDLE EASTERN WORLD, 600-1500
THE ASIAN WORLD, 600-1500
AN AGE OF EMPIRES, 1200-1750
AN AGE OF VOYAGES, 1350-1600
AN AGE OF SCIENCE AND REVOLUTIONS, 1600-1800

"The liveliest, most realistic, most well-received American history series ever written for children."
– *Los Angeles Times*

A HISTORY OF US
JOY HAKIM
THE FIRST AMERICANS
MAKING THIRTEEEN COLONIES
FROM COLONIES TO COUNTRY
THE NEW NATION
LIBERTY FOR ALL?
WAR, TERRIBLE WAR
RECONSTRUCTING AMERICA
AN AGE OF EXTREMES
WAR, PEACE, AND ALL THAT JAZZ
ALL THE PEOPLE

FOR MORE INFORMATION, VISIT US AT WWW.OUP.COM

New from Oxford University Press
Reading History, by Janet Allen
ISBN 0-19-516595-0 hc   0-19-516596-9 pb

"*Reading History* is a great idea. I highly recommend this book."
–Dennis Denenberg, *Professor of Elementary and Early Childhood Education, Millersville University*

NOTE TO THE TEACHER

Dear Fellow Educator:

How do we realize our hopes and dreams? How do we face the challenges of everyday life? Everyone—old and young alike—asks such questions at one time or another. One place to look for answers is in the lives of people in the past. In history we find ordinary people building cathedrals and mosques, conducting trade over thousands of miles, eking out a living through agriculture and crafts, and dreaming dreams of creating vast empires. This series brings you their stories.

As educators, we want to present these stories as part of a living past—and the authors of our books aim to provide you with the materials to do just that. We offer ways to make the past come alive with vivid images in full color, lively accounts of actual people, and maps to show young readers where these people lived and how they traveled the world. Heroes tell us in their own words of their noblest hopes; villains show us their cruelty. Ordinary folks face the plague and young boys set out in creaky ships on dangerous seas. This series helps you show young adults the fullness of the past and the grand achievements that make up our heritage.

We all know that our task does not stop at presenting the *story* of the past. We must also teach our students the *skills* vital to understanding history and to becoming informed citizens. These books are designed to help you train students to think critically about human opinions, prejudices, and programs for the future. The many voices from historical actors in the series provide opportunities for students to come to terms with burning issues of bias and point of view.

You and I share not only great hopes for the future but also the daily challenges of teaching. In addition to the stories, images, quotes, maps, timelines, and young adult bibliographies of the books themselves, the series includes instructional guides with tested ideas for teaching the medieval and early modern world. These guides are filled with exercises, classroom activities, and daily lessons based on specific chapters in each book. They show additional, practical ways to make critical thinking an integral part of your work in world history.

The authors of the student books and the supporting instructional materials bring you and your students the very latest thinking about what world history is. We urge you to tell us how their presentation of this vital, emerging field works with your students. Good history, like the creation of civilization itself, depends on our common effort!

Bonnie G. Smith
General Editor

THE MEDIEVAL & EARLY MODERN WORLD PROGRAM

I. STUDENT EDITION

- Engaging, friendly narrative
- A wide range of primary sources in every chapter
- The authority of Oxford scholarship
- Period illustrations and specially commissioned maps

II. TEACHING GUIDE

- Wide range of activities and classroom approaches
- Strategies for universal access and improving literacy (ELL, struggling readers, advanced learners)
- Multiple assessment tools

III. STUDENT STUDY GUIDE

- Exercises correlated to Student Edition and Teaching Guide
- Portfolio approach
- Activities for every level of learning
- Literacy through reading and writing

PRIMARY SOURCES AND REFERENCE VOLUME

- Broad selection of primary sources in each subject area
- Ideal resource for in-class exercises and unit projects

TEACHING GUIDE: KEY FEATURES

The Teaching Guides organize each *Medieval & Early Modern World* book into chapter-based lessons of six (6) pages each, preceded by a special section that includes one longer-term project per chapter. These projects are cross-curricular, designed for mixed-group participation, and suitable for a wide range of learning styles. They can be used for teacher and student self- or peer assessment with the rubrics at the back of this Teaching Guide.

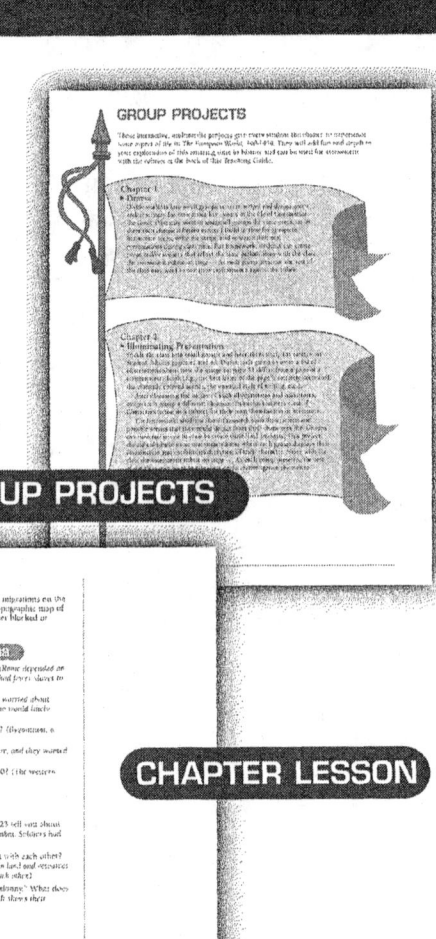

GROUP PROJECTS
Engaging, creative projects for group work on a wide variety of inviting topics

CHAPTER LESSONS
Teaching strategies and suggestions that address curriculum and that link with Student Study Guide and Student Edition

TESTS AND BLACKLINE MASTERS (BLMS)
Reproducible tests; map skills, primary sources, and document-based questions (DBQs) for assessment, homework, or classroom projects

TEACHING GUIDE: CHAPTER LESSONS

Teaching guides are organized so that you can easily find the information you need.

CHAPTER SUMMARY AND PERFORMANCE OBJECTIVES
The Chapter Summary gives an overview of the information in the chapter. The Performance Objectives are the three or four important goals students should achieve in the chapter. Accomplishing these goals will help students master the information in the book as well as meet standards for the course.

BUILDING BACKGROUND
This section connects students to the chapter they are about to read. Students may be asked to use what they know to make predictions about the text, preview the images in the chapter, or connect modern life with the historical subject matter.

VOCABULARY
A word list for every chapter defines difficult words and key curricular terms and recaps glossary entries.

CHAPTER 1

BELIEVERS AND BARBARIANS: THE END OF THE ROMAN EMPIRE
PAGES 20–33

FOR HOMEWORK
Student Study Guide pages
Chapter 1   13-16

CHAPTER SUMMARY
Both external and internal problems weakened Rome. When Constantine the Great converted to Christianity he moved the capital east to a city later renamed Constantinople. The empire gradually divided into the Eastern Empire and the Western Empire, each with its own version of Christianity. In 410 the Visigoths conquered Rome. However, Rome's legacy lived on through Latin, government structures, and architecture.

PERFORMANCE OBJECTIVES
▶ To identify the factors that threatened the Roman Empire
▶ To define and evaluate the key events in the life and rule of Constantine
▶ To identify the lasting contributions of Rome

BUILDING BACKGROUND
Ask students to preview the chapter by reading the headings and subheadings, studying the photographs and captions, and examining the map. Based on the preview, work with students to compile a list of questions about the fall of Rome and the rise of Christianity. As students locate the answers to their questions, have them record them on the list.

VOCABULARY
empire huge region of varied cultures under the control of one government
citizen person owing loyalty to and entitled to protection by a state or a nation
Christianity the religion based on the life and teachings of Jesus Christ
convert person who has been convinced to change from one religion to another
barbarian name given to outsiders by the Romans, who viewed them as uncivilized
drought a long period of very low rainfall

As needed, have students consult the glossary to define the following words: *bishop, centralize, council, excommunicate, heretic, New Testament, persecution, plunder, saint*

CAST OF CHARACTERS
Augustine (aw-GUS-teen), Roman nobleman who converted to Christianity
Constantine the Great (KON-stun-teen), First Roman emperor to convert to Christianity
Visigoths (VIH-zih-goths), Arian Christian Germanic tribe that attacked Rome in 410

WORKING WITH PRIMARY SOURCES
Point out the quotation from Ambrose in Student Edition page 23. If necessary, refer students to the glossary, and explain that excommunicated means to be deprived of the right of church membership by the church leadership. Discuss what the quotation reveals about early Christian beliefs. Why do you think Ambrose asked the emperor to repent? Invite students to read more of Ambrose's letter to the emperor, written in 390, at http://www.fordham.edu/halsall/source/ambrose-let51.html

28 / CHAPTER 1

WORKING WITH PRIMARY SOURCES
A major feature of *The Medieval & Early Modern World* is the opportunity to read about history through the words and images of the people who lived it. Each book includes excerpts from the best sources from these ancient civilizations, giving the narrative an immediacy that is difficult to match in secondary sources. Students can read further in these sources on their own or in small groups using the accompanying *Primary Sources and Reference Volume*. The Teaching Guide recommends activities so students of all skill levels can appreciate the ways people from the past saw themselves, their ideas and values, and their fears and dreams.

8

LINKING DISCIPLINES

Art Have students research examples of arches, roads, and aqueducts constructed throughout the Roman Empire. You might want to display a map of the Roman Empire on the wall. Instruct students to research in a library or on the Internet to find examples of Roman architecture. Have them sketch or print copies, write brief captions, and affix them on the map. Ask students to identify similarities between these ancient structures and familiar modern structures.

LITERACY TIPS

In addition to using the suggestions in the Supporting Learning and Extending Learning sections, refer back frequently to pages 20–23 for strategies and advice from a literacy coach.

WRITING

Persuasive Letter Have students review the events of Augustine's life as described in the chapter. Next have them write a persuasive letter or sermon that he might have addressed to non-Christians to describe his conversion and persuade them of his beliefs. What figurative language might he use to compel them? What experiences would he share from his life? *(Assessment: students incorporate supporting detail and language from the chapter. Their letters should also represent the tensions between Christians and non-Christians.)*

SUPPORTING LEARNING

English Language Learners Help students recognize and use multiple-meaning words. Using the paragraphs on Student Edition page 27, identify and define such words as letters, beat, torn, and passage. Help students use context clues and their prior knowledge to figure out which meaning is being used. Ask volunteers to suggest sentences using various meanings of the words.

Struggling Readers Have students complete the Sequence of Events Chart at the back of the guide to show how one event led to another, and then another, in the history of early Christianity. For example, they can list how Christianity's spread led to the executions of Christians, and so on. Remind them to look for key dates, such as Constantine's conversion in 312.

EXTENDING LEARNING

Enrichment Invite students to learn more about one of these cities as they are today: Rome, Carthage, or Constantinople. Direct students to use search engines...

GEOGRAPHY CONNECTION

Movement Have students trace the routes of the Germanic migrations on the map on page 31. They may want to compare the map with a topographic map of Europe to locate features, such as mountains or rivers that either blocked or aided the movement of these peoples.

READING COMPREHENSION QUESTIONS

1. Why did economic and social conditions worsen in Rome? *(Rome depended on slaves to produce food. When the empire stopped expanding, it had fewer slaves to do the work.)*
2. Why did Roman authorities fear the early Christians? *(They worried about uprisings. Christianity was becoming popular among people who would likely rebel: the poor in cities, slaves, and soldiers.)*
3. Where did Constantine locate the new capital of the empire? *(Byzantium, a small Greek city near Asia Minor)*
4. Why did the Huns migrate west? *(Drought ruined their pasture, and they wanted better lives for themselves.)*
5. What happened after the Visigoths advanced on Rome in 410? *(The western emperor fled, and the Visigoths plundered Rome.)*

CRITICAL THINKING QUESTIONS

1. What does the image of the shield on Student Edition page 23 tell you about warfare during this time? *(Warfare included hand-to-hand combat. Soldiers had access to iron for added protection.)*
2. Why were the Romans, Germanic tribes, and Huns in conflict with each other? *(They wanted to either keep control of land and resources, or gain land and resources from the other groups. They fought rather than cooperate with each other.)*
3. One Goth observer described the Huns as "small, foul, and skinny." What does it say about the Goths' view of the Huns during this time? *(It shows their negative opinion of the Goths.)*

SOCIAL SCIENCES

Military History Attila the Hun is still famous today for his resilience and brutality. Have students research his attack on Rome using the Internet or library resources. Next have them use their history journals to write from Attila's point of view a series of short diary entries describing his advance toward Rome.

READING AND LANGUAGE ARTS

Reading Nonfiction As students read the text, have them use the strategy "list/group/label" to work with the vocabulary. First have them individually list words that relate to different cultures or religious groups as they read. Then have students form groups of three and share their lists. Next, ask the groups to identify and name at least five categories in which to put the words, and sort them into the categories to which they best belong. Finally, have each small group display their choices and share the reasons behind them with the class.

Using Language Direct students' attention to the quotation from Ambrose on page 27. Have them draw in their history journals an image it brings to mind. With partners, students can share images and discuss why Ambrose might have described the church the way he did. Next, have partners consider what the "raging sea" represents. As a whole class, speculate about the effect of his words on both Christians and on non-Christians.

THE EUROPEAN WORLD, 400–1450 | 29

WRITING
Each chapter has a suggestion for a specific writing assignment. These assignments can help students meet state requirements in writing as well improve their skills.

SUPPORTING LEARNING AND EXTENDING LEARNING
Suggestions for students of varying abilities and learning styles: advanced learners, struggling readers, auditory/visual/tactile learners, and English language learners. These may be individual, partner, or group activities. *(For more on reading and literacy, see pp. 16-19.)*

GEOGRAPHY CONNECTION
Each chapter has a Geography Connection to strengthen students' map skills as well as their understanding of how geography affects human civilization. One of the five themes of geography is highlighted in each chapter.

READING COMPREHENSION AND CRITICAL THINKING QUESTIONS
The reading comprehension questions are general enough to allow free-flowing class or small group discussion, yet specific enough to be used for oral or written assessment of students' grasp of the important information. The critical thinking questions are intended to engage students in a deeper analysis of the text and can also be used for oral or written assessment.

SOCIAL SCIENCES ACTIVITIES
These activities connect the subject matter in the Student Edition with economics, civics, and science, technology, and society.

READING AND LANGUAGE ARTS
Some activities can facilitate the development of nonfiction reading strategies. Others help students' appreciation of fiction and poetry, focusing on word choice, description, and figurative language.

TEACHING GUIDE: CHAPTER SIDEBARS

Icons quickly help identify key concepts, facts, activities, and assessment activities in the sidebars.

▶ Cast of Characters
This sidebar points out and identifies significant personalities in the chapter. Pronunciation guides are included where necessary.

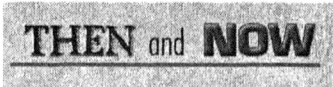

▶ Then and Now
This feature provides interesting facts and ideas about the ancient civilization and relates it to the modern world. This may be an aspect of government still in use today, word origins of common modern expressions, physical reminders of the past, and other features. You can use this item simply to promote interest in the subject matter or as a springboard to other research.

▶ Linking Disciplines
This feature offers opportunities to investigate other subject areas that relate to the material in the Student Edition: math, science, arts, and health. Specific areas of these subjects are emphasized: **Math** (arithmetic, algebra, geometry, data, statistics); **Science** (life science, earth science, physical science); **Arts** (music, arts, dance, drama, architecture); **Health** (personal health, world health).

▶ For Homework
A quick glance links you to additional activities in the Student Study Guide that can be assigned as homework.

ASSESSMENT

The Medieval & Early Modern World program intentionally omits from the Student Edition the kinds of section, chapter, and unit questions that are used to review and assess learning in standard textbooks. It is the purpose of the series to engage readers in learning—and loving—history written as good literature. Rather than interrupting student reading and enjoyment, all assessment instruments for the series have been placed in the Teaching Guides.

▶ **CHAPTER TESTS**
A reproducible chapter test follows each chapter in this Teaching Guide. These tests will help you assess students' mastery of the content addressed in each chapter. These tests measure a variety of cognitive and analytical skills, particularly comprehension, critical thinking, and expository writing through multiple choice, short answer, and essay questions.
An answer key for the chapter tests is provided at the end of the Teaching Guide.

▶ **WRAP-UP TEST**
After the last chapter test you will find a wrap-up test consisting of 10 essay questions that evaluate students' ability to synthesize and express what they've learned about the civilization under study. Depending upon your class, you may want to consider assigning the questions as a takehome or open-book test.

▶ **RUBRICS**
The rubrics at the back of this Teaching Guide will help you assess students' written work, oral presentations, and group projects. They include a Scoring Rubric based on standards for good writing and effective cooperative learning. In addition, a simplified hand-out is provided, plus a form for evaluating group projects and a Library/Media Center Research Log to help students focus and evaluate their research. Students can also evaluate their own work using these rubrics.

▶ **BLACKLINE MASTERS (BLMs)**
Two blackline masters follow each chapter in the Teaching Guide. These BLMs are reproducible pages for you to use as in-class activities or homework exercises. Assigning primary source blackline masters to groups or partners is strongly encouraged, as this material may be quite challenging to some students. They can also be used for assessment as needed.

▶ **ADDITIONAL ASSESSMENT ACTIVITIES**
The Group Project sections and Chapter Lessons of this Teaching Guide provide numerous activities and projects that have been designated as additional assessment opportunities, using the rubrics at the back of this Guide.

USING THE STUDENT STUDY GUIDE FOR ASSESSMENT

▶ Study Guide Activities
Assignments in the Student Study Guide correspond with those in the Teaching Guide. If needed, these Student Study Guide activities can be used for assessment.

▶ Portfolio Approach
Student Study Guide pages can be removed from the workbook and turned in for grading. When the pages are returned, they can be part of the students' individual history journals. Have students keep a 3-ring binder portfolio of Study Guide pages alongside writing projects and other activities.

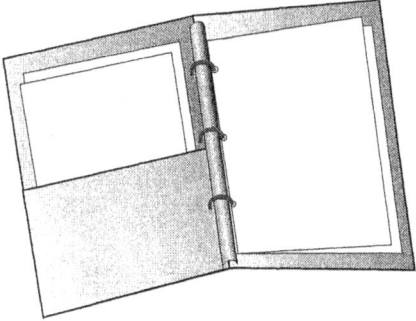

STUDENT STUDY GUIDE: KEY FEATURES

The Student Study Guide works as both standalone instructional material and as a support to the Student Edition and this Teaching Guide. Certain activities encourage informal small-group or family participation. These features make it an effective teaching tool:

Flexibility

You can use the Study Guide in the classroom, with individuals or small groups, or send it home for homework. You can distribute the entire guide to students; however, the pages are perforated so you can remove and distribute only the pertinent lessons.

A page on reports and special projects directs students to the "Further Reading" resource in the student edition. This feature gives students general guidance on doing research and devising independent study projects of their own.

FACSIMILE SPREAD
The Study Guide begins with a facsimile spread from the Student Edition. This spread gives reading strategies and highlights key features: captions, primary sources, sidebars, headings, etymologies. The spread supplies the contextualization students need to fully understand the material.

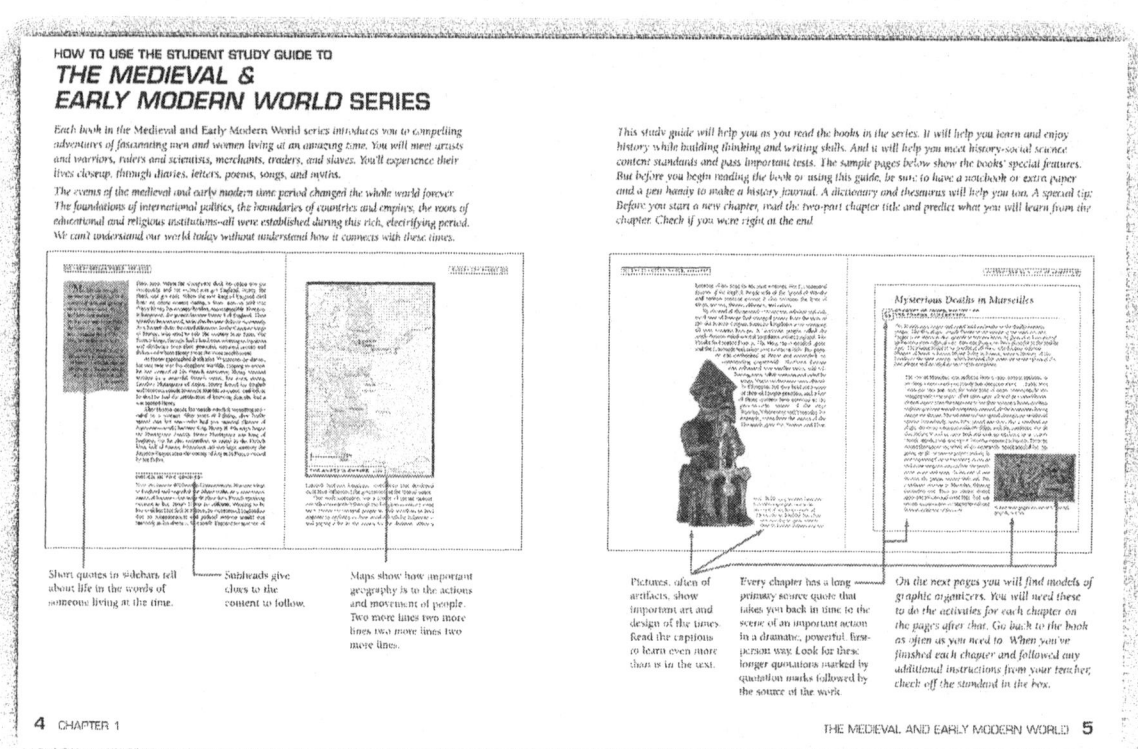

Portfolio Approach

The Study Guide pages are three-hole-punched so they can be integrated with notebook paper in a looseleaf binder. This history journal or portfolio can become both a record of content mastery and an outlet for each student's unique creative expression. Responding to prompts, students can write poetry or songs, plays and character sketches, create storyboards or cartoons, or construct multi-layered timelines.

The portfolio approach gives students unlimited opportunities for practice in areas that need strengthening. Students can share their journals and compare their work. And the Study Guide pages in the portfolio make a valuable assessment tool for you. The portfolio is an ongoing record of performance that can be reviewed and graded periodically.

GRAPHIC ORGANIZERS

This feature contains reduced models of seven graphic organizers referenced frequently in the study guide. Using these devices will help students organize the material so it is meaningful to them. (Full-size reproducibles of each graphic organizer are provided at the back of this Teaching Guide.) These graphic organizers include: outline, main idea map, K-W-L chart (What I Know, What I Want to Know, What I Learned), Venn diagram, timeline, sequence of events chart, and T-chart.

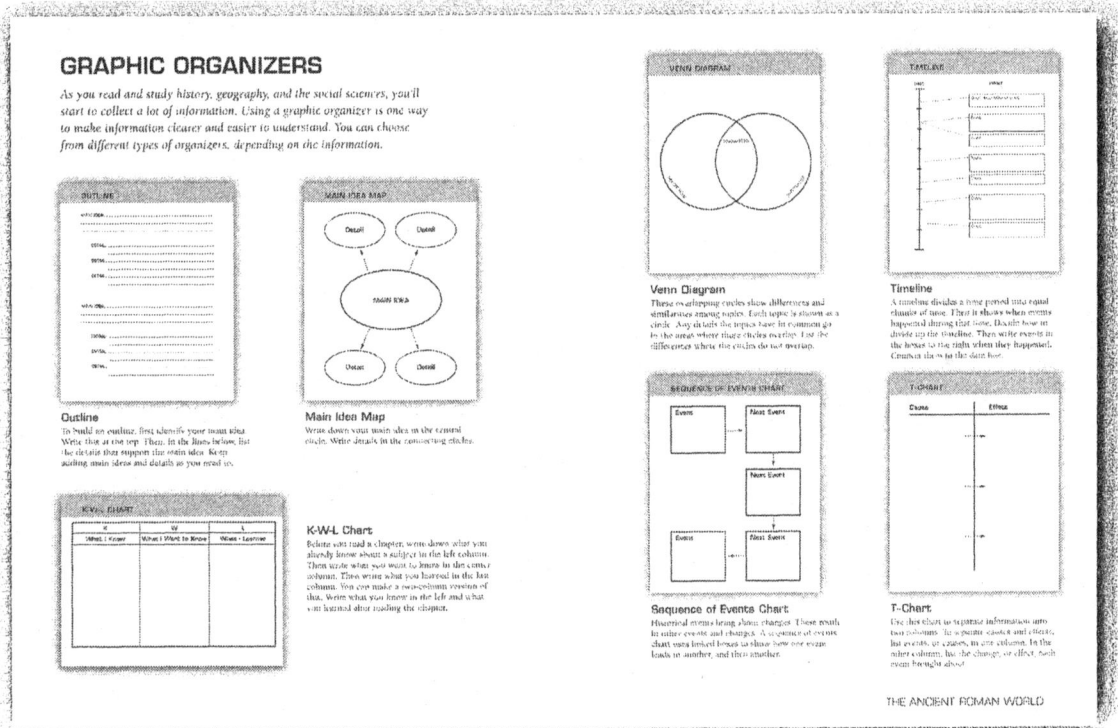

STUDENT STUDY GUIDE: CHAPTER LESSONS

Each chapter lesson is designed to draw students into the subject matter. Recurring features and exercises challenge their knowledge and allow them to practice valuable analysis and English language arts skills. Activities in the Teaching Guide and Student Study Guide complement but do not duplicate each other. Together they offer a wide range of class work, group projects, and opportunities for further study and assessment that can be tailored to all ability levels.

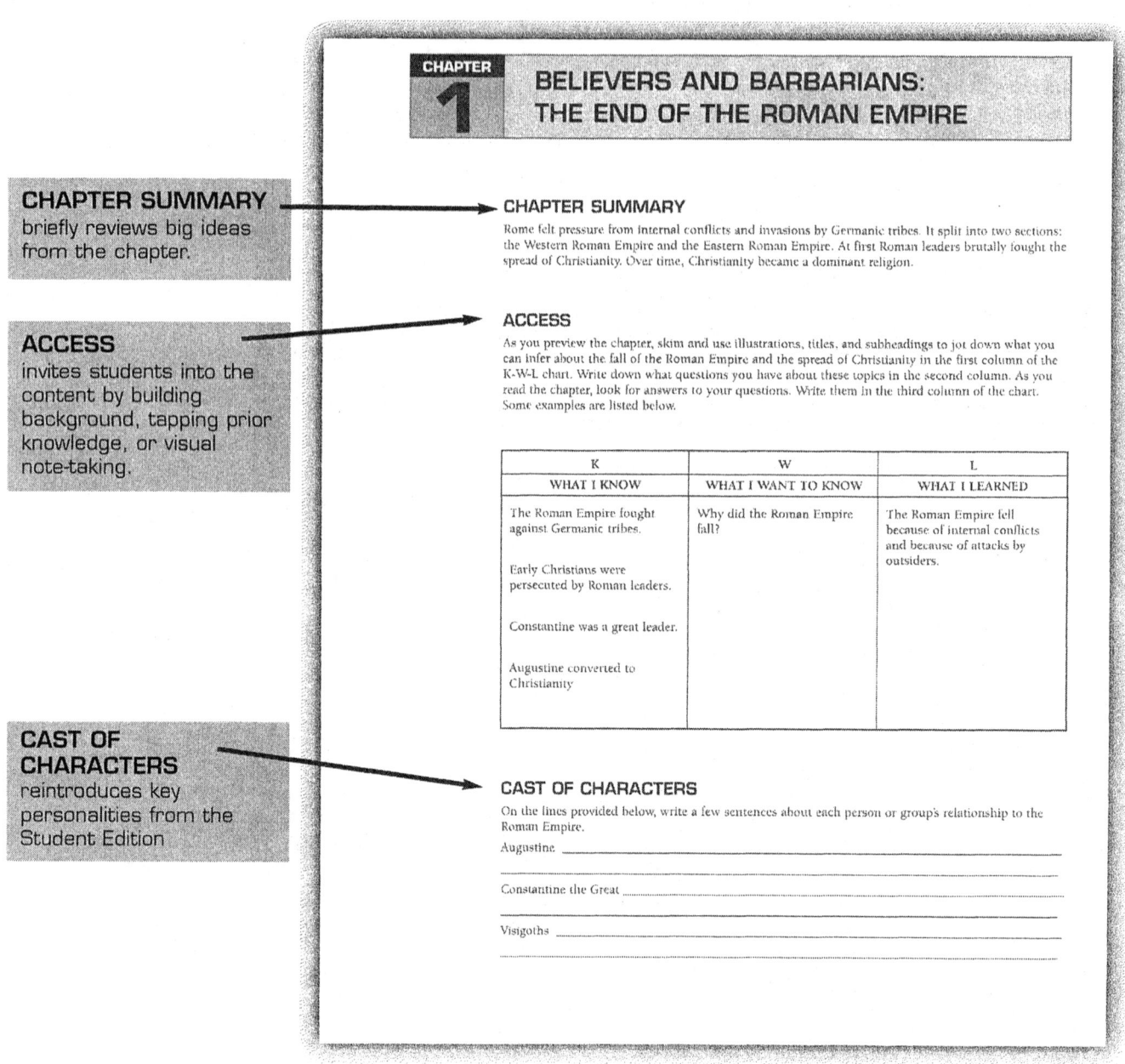

CHAPTER SUMMARY briefly reviews big ideas from the chapter.

ACCESS invites students into the content by building background, tapping prior knowledge, or visual note-taking.

CAST OF CHARACTERS reintroduces key personalities from the Student Edition

CHAPTER 1: BELIEVERS AND BARBARIANS: THE END OF THE ROMAN EMPIRE

CHAPTER SUMMARY
Rome felt pressure from internal conflicts and invasions by Germanic tribes. It split into two sections: the Western Roman Empire and the Eastern Roman Empire. At first Roman leaders brutally fought the spread of Christianity. Over time, Christianity became a dominant religion.

ACCESS
As you preview the chapter, skim and use illustrations, titles, and subheadings to jot down what you can infer about the fall of the Roman Empire and the spread of Christianity in the first column of the K-W-L chart. Write down what questions you have about these topics in the second column. As you read the chapter, look for answers to your questions. Write them in the third column of the chart. Some examples are listed below.

K	W	L
WHAT I KNOW	WHAT I WANT TO KNOW	WHAT I LEARNED
The Roman Empire fought against Germanic tribes.	Why did the Roman Empire fall?	The Roman Empire fell because of internal conflicts and because of attacks by outsiders.
Early Christians were persecuted by Roman leaders.		
Constantine was a great leader.		
Augustine converted to Christianity		

CAST OF CHARACTERS
On the lines provided below, write a few sentences about each person or group's relationship to the Roman Empire.

Augustine _____

Constantine the Great _____

Visigoths _____

14

WORD BANK
Choose five of the six words below and use them to write a paragraph about the Roman Empire in your history journal.
1. (empire, citizen)
2. (Christianity, convert)
3. (barbarian, drought)

WORD PLAY
Look up the word *citizen* in the dictionary. Find out its origin. Explain how the word's original meaning relates to its current meaning.

WITH A PARENT OR PARTNER
One of the forces of Germanic migration was a drought in the fourth century. With a parent or partner, research other famous or catastrophic droughts from another time period in history. Create and illustrate a chart that contrasts life in the area, community, or culture before and after the drought. Display your chart in the classroom.

CRITICAL THINKING
CONTRASTING CULTURES
The end of the Roman Empire was a turbulent time. Descriptions of the Romans, the Christians, and the barbarians clashed...
contrasts include however...

CONTRAST	
The ancient Roman religion... belief in many gods. Christianity... based on the belief in one...	

Look at pages 28 and 29 in... Roman/Mediterranean civil... details for each culture. T... partner.

Category	
Environment	

WORKING WITH PRIMARY SOURCES
Read the law of the Franks, a Germanic people, on Student Edition page 29.

> If anyone has assaulted and plundered a free person, and it be proved on him, he shall be [fined] 2,500 dinars, which make 63 shillings. If a Roman has plundered a Frank... above law shall be observed. But if a Frank has plundered a Roman, he shall be [fined] 35 shillings.

IDENTIFYING POINT OF VIEW
The first Germanic kings copied the Roman practice of writing codes of law. In the late 400s, for example, King Euric, the Visigoth king of Gaul, wrote the Germanic customary law into code.

1. What crimes does the law address?

2. Why do you think customary laws, or laws based on tradition and custom, were eventually written down?

3. What does the law show about the Franks' attitudes toward the Romans at this time?

4. Do you know of any other laws in history that showed bias toward one group of people in a society? Give examples.

WRITE ABOUT IT
In your history journal, write an essay in which you invent a rule or law for your community...

ALL OVER THE MAP
Directions: Follow the steps below to complete the map.

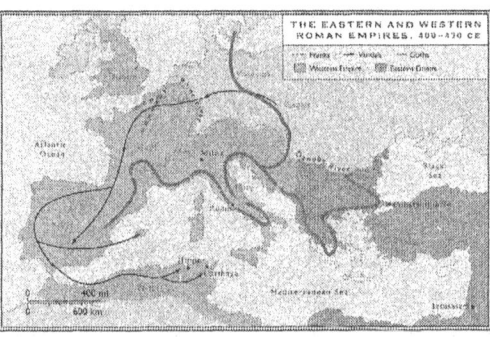

- Scan pages 28-31 to find information on the migrations of the Franks, Vandals, Visigoths, and the Huns.
- Look at a physical-political map of modern Europe and Asia in an atlas.
- Write the mountain ranges on the map here.
- Label the Balkan Peninsula.
- Label Central Asia.
- Draw a line showing the approximate migration route of the Huns.
- Add the line representing the Huns and the term *Huns* to the key.
- Write a paragraph in your history journal that answers these questions:
  - What were the natural boundaries of the Roman Empire's northern frontier?
  - What physical features affected the migrations of each group?
- Give your map a title that explains what the map shows.

WORD BANK reintroduces key curricular terms and difficult words from the Student Edition.

CRITICAL THINKING exercises draw on such thinking skills as establishing cause and effect, making inferences, comparing and contrasting, identifying main ideas and details, and other analytical process.

WORKING WITH PRIMARY SOURCES invites students to read primary sources closely. Exercises include DBQ's, evaluating point of view, and writing.

WRITE ABOUT IT A writing assignment may stem from a vocabulary word, a historical event, or a primary source. The assignment can be a newspaper article, letter, short essay, a scene with dialogue, a diary entry.

ALL OVER THE MAP uses engaging map skills activities to help students understand geography's crucial role in shaping history.

IMPROVING LITERACY WITH THE MEDIEVAL & EARLY MODERN WORLD

The books in this series are written in a lively, narrative style to inspire a love of reading history. English language learners and struggling readers are given special consideration within the program's exercises and activities. And students who love to read and learn will also benefit from the program's rich and varied material. Following are strategies to make sure each and every student gets the most out of the subjects you will teach through *The Medieval & Early Modern World*.

ENGLISH LANGUAGE LEARNERS

For English learners to achieve academic success, the instructional considerations for teachers include two mandates:

- Help them attain grade level, content area knowledge, and academic language.
- Provide for the development of English language proficiency.

To accomplish these goals, you should plan lessons that reflect the student's level of English proficiency. Students progress through five developmental levels as they increase in language proficiency:

> Beginning and Early Intermediate (*grade level material will be mostly incomprehensible, students need a great deal of teacher support*)
>
> Intermediate (*grade level work will be a challenge*)
>
> Early Advanced and Advanced (*close to grade level reading and writing, students continue to need support*)

Refer to your state's ELD Standards for information about language proficiency at each level. The books in this program are written at the intermediate level. However, you can still use the lesson plans for students of different levels by using the strategies below:

Tap Prior Knowledge
What students know about the topic will help determine your next steps for instruction. Using K-W-L charts, brainstorming, and making lists are ways to find out what they know. English learners bring a rich cultural diversity into the classroom. By sharing what they know, students can connect their knowledge and experiences to the course.

Set the Context
Use different tools to make new information understandable. These can be images, artifacts, maps, timelines, illustrations, charts, videos, or graphic organizers. Techniques such as role-playing and story-boarding can also be helpful. Speak in shorter sentences, with careful enunciation, expanded explanations, repetitions, and paraphrasing. Use fewer idiomatic expressions.

Show—Don't Just Tell
English learners often get lost as they listen to directions, explanations, lectures, and discussions. By showing students what is expected, you can help them participate more fully in classroom activities. Students need to be shown how to use the graphic organizers in this guide and the mini versions in the student study guide, as well as other blackline masters for note-taking and practice. An overhead transparency with whole or small groups is also effective.

Use the Text
Because of unfamiliar words, students will need help. Teach them to preview the chapter using text features (headings, bold print, sidebars, italics). See the suggestions in the facsimile of the Student Edition, shown on pages 6–7 of the Student Study Guide. Show students organizing structures such as cause and effect or comparing and contrasting. Have students read to each other in pairs. Encourage them to share their history journals with each other. Use Read Aloud/Think Aloud, perhaps with an overhead transparency. Help them create word banks, charts, and graphic organizers. Discuss the main idea after reading.

Check for Understanding
Rather than simply ask students if they understand, stop frequently and ask them to paraphrase or expand on what you just said. Such techniques will give you a much clearer assessment of their understanding.

Provide for Interaction
As students interact with the information and speak their thoughts, their content knowledge and academic language skills improve. Increase interaction in the classroom through cooperative learning, small group work, and partner share. By working and talking with others, students can practice asking and answering questions.

Use Appropriate Assessment
When modifying the instruction, you will also need to modify the assessment. Multiple choice, true and false, and other criterion reference tests are suitable, but consider changing test format and structure. English learners are constantly improving their language proficiency in their oral and written responses, but they are often grammatically incorrect. Remember to be thoughtful and fair about giving students credit for their content knowledge and use of academic language, even if their English isn't perfect.

STRUGGLING READERS

Some students struggle to understand the information presented in a textbook. The following strategies for content-area reading can help students improve their ability to make comparisons, sequence events, determine importance, summarize, evaluate, synthesize, analyze, and solve problems.

Build Knowledge of Genre
Both the fiction and narrative nonfiction genres are incorporated into *The Medieval & Early Modern World*. This combination of genres makes the text interesting and engaging. But teachers must be sure students can identify and use the organizational structures of both genres.

Fiction	Nonfiction
Each chapter is a story	Content: historical information
Setting: historical time and place	Organizational structure: cause/effect, sequence of events, problem/solution
Characters: historical figures	Other features: maps, timelines, sidebars, photographs, primary sources
Plot: problems, roadblocks, and resolutions	

In addition, the textbook has a wealth of the text features of nonfiction: bold and italic print, sidebars, headings and subheadings, labels, captions, and "signal words" such as *first*, *next*, and *finally*. Teaching these organizational structures and text features is essential for struggling readers.

Build Background

Having background information about a topic makes reading about it so much easier. When students lack background information, teachers can preteach or "front load" concepts and vocabulary, using a variety of instructional techniques. Conduct a chapter or book walk, looking at titles, headings, and other text features to develop a big picture of the content. Focus on new vocabulary words during the "walk" and create a word bank with illustrations for future reference. Read aloud key passages and discuss the meaning. Focus on the timeline and maps to help students develop a sense of time and place. Show a video, go to a website, and have trade books and magazines on the topic available for student exploration.

Comprehension Strategies

While reading, successful readers are predicting, making connections, monitoring, visualizing, questioning, inferring, and summarizing. Struggling readers have a harder time with these "in the head" processes. The following strategies will help these students construct meaning from the text until they are able to do it on their own.

PREDICT: Before reading, conduct a picture and text feature "tour" of the chapter to make predictions. Ask students if they remember if this has ever happened before, to predict what might happen this time.

MAKE CONNECTIONS: Help students relate content to their background (text to text, text to self, and text to the world).

MONITOR AND CONFIRM: Encourage students to stop reading when they come across an unknown word, phrase, or concept. In their notebooks, have them make a note of text they don't understand and ask for clarification or figure it out. While this activity slows down reading at first, it is effective in improving skills over time.

VISUALIZE: Students benefit from imagining the events described in a story. Sketching scenes, story-boarding, role-playing, and looking for sensory details all help students with this strategy.

INFER: Help students look beyond the literal meaning of a text to understand deeper meanings. Graphic organizers and discussions provide opportunities to broaden their understanding. Looking closely at the "why" of historical events helps students infer.

QUESTION AND DISCUSS: Have students jot down their questions as they read, and then share them during discussions. Or have students come up with the type of questions they think a teacher would ask. Over time students will develop more complex inferential questions, which lead to group discussions. Questioning and discussing also helps students see ideas from multiple perspectives and draw conclusions, both critical skills for understanding history.

DETERMINE IMPORTANCE: Teach students how to decide what is most important from all the facts and details in nonfiction. After reading for an overall understanding, they can go back to highlight important ideas, words, and phrases. Clues for determining importance include bold or italic print, signal words, and other text features. A graphic organizer such as a main idea map also helps.

Teach and Practice Decoding Strategies

Rather than simply defining an unfamiliar word, teach struggling readers decoding strategies:

- Have them look at the prefix, suffix, and root to help figure out the new word.
- Look for words they know within the word.
- Use the context for clues, and read further or reread.

ADVANCED LEARNERS

Every classroom has students who finish the required assignments and then want additional challenges. Fortunately, the very nature of history and social science offers a wide range of opportunities for students to explore topics in greater depth. Encourage them to come up with their own ideas for an additional assignment. Determine the final product, its presentation, and a timeline for completion.

▶ Research

Students can develop in-depth understanding through seeking information, exploring ideas, asking and answering questions, making judgments, considering points of view, and evaluating actions and events. They will need access to a wide range of resource materials: the Internet, maps, encyclopedias, trade books, magazines, dictionaries, artifacts, newspapers, museum catalogues, brochures, and the library. See the "Further Reading" section at the end of the Student Edition for good jumping-off points.

▶ Projects

You can encourage students to capitalize on their strengths as learners (visual, verbal, kinesthetic, or musical) or to try a new way of responding. Students can prepare a debate or write a persuasive paper, play, skit, poem, song, dance, game, puzzle, or biography. They can create an alphabet book on the topic, film a video, do a book talk, or illustrate a book. They can render charts, graphs, or other visual representations. Allow for creativity and support students' thinking.

Cheryl A. Caldera, M.A.
Literacy Coach

GROUP PROJECTS

These interactive, multimedia projects give every student the chance to experience some aspect of life in *The African & Middle Eastern World, 600–1500*. They will add fun and depth to your exploration of this amazing time in history and can be used for assessment with the rubrics at the back of this Teaching Guide.

Chapter 1
▶ **On the Road to Mecca**

Divide students into partners and direct each pair to determine which person will take the part of a caravan driver and which will be a member of a Bedouin tribe. Ask students to reread Chapter 1 together, keeping in mind the roles they will play, and paying close attention to the relationship between these two groups of people. For homework, students can do further research on the Internet or at the library to find out more about the character they are to play and that person's relationship with the other character. They can also collect props they think would be appropriate for their character. Have students use class time to brainstorm ideas and write a skit in their history journals in which the two characters will interact. The skits should include introductory information on each character and background information on the relationship between the two groups they represent. Encourage students to practice their skits. This project could culminate with students performing their skits for the class. Share with the class the assessment rubric in the back of this guide. As each pair performs, the rest of the class may want to rate the performances against the rubric.

Chapter 2
▶ **An Exclusive Magazine Interview**

Divide students into partners. Direct students to review the chapter and take notes in their history journals as they read about the details of Muhammad's life and teachings. Then invite students to discuss the points about Muhammad's life and teachings that they would like to know more about. Have them formulate questions they would ask the Prophet if they could interview him. For homework, have students do further research about their questions on the Internet or at the library. Encourage them to write additional questions based on any new information they find. Then allow students class time to formulate the answers, based on their research, that they think Muhammad would give for the questions they have written. This project could culminate with students using their word-processing skills to publish their interviews as would be seen in a news magazine. Interviews can be made available for the class to read. Share with the class the assessment rubric in the back of this guide.

Chapter 3
▸ Eyewitness Account

During the time of Islamic expansion, there were many conflicts which allowed Islam to spread throughout the Sassanid Empire in the east and all the way to Spain in the west. Students can work in pairs to choose one area of conflict to research. They can use the information in the chapter as well as information on the Internet and in the library. Areas students can consider in their research could include, but not be limited to, methods of attack, length of the conflict, how the conflict ended, and who was involved. After students have collected their information, they can write an eyewitness account from the perspective of someone involved in the conflict, such as a Muslim warrior, a member of the opposing army, or a citizen of the place being attacked. This project should culminate with the students presenting their eyewitness accounts to the class. Share with the class the assessment rubric in the back of this guide.

Chapter 4
▸ Help Wanted

An ad has been placed in the Islamic Empire Newspaper looking for a new leader for the Islamic Empire. Many strong candidates are expected to apply. Students can work in small groups and research one of the following candidates: Abu Bakr, Umar, Uthman, Ali, or Muawiyah. The groups can collect information from Chapters 3 and 4 in the student edition and then do further research for homework. Students can look for information that falls into the categories that can be found on a résumé, such as education, work experience, qualifications, related skills, etc. Once students have gathered the necessary information, they can work as a group to write a résumé for the person they have researched. This project could culminate with a job interview, during which the teacher and fellow students interview a group, asking questions related to how this person would perform the job of leader of the Islamic Empire and what this person's goals would be for the Empire. Share with the class the assessment rubric in the back of this guide.

Chapter 5
▶ Travel Brochure

Ibn Battuta traveled all over the Islamic world, and although his travels took place hundreds of years after the events discussed in this chapter, what he saw resulted from these events. He wrote about his travels and observations, which give people today a good look at how the Islamic Empire looked during his time. Students can work in pairs to create a travel brochure for the Islamic Empire that Ibn Battuta observed. They will need to research some of the important buildings and sites that could be found throughout the empire, such as the palace at Baghdad, the palaces of the caliphs, and the many mosques. Pairs of students can use the writings of Ibn Battuta or other sources to write a travel brochure with descriptions of the important places for a traveler to the region to visit. Students can also include pictures of these places, as well as creative recommendations for lodging and restaurants. Each pair of students can present their travel brochures, and the brochures can be displayed in the classroom for students to reference. Share with the class the assessment rubric in the back of this guide.

Chapter 6
▶ Debate

The chapter states that the Abbasid caliphs encouraged discussion and debate about the Quran and the hadiths. Explain that the class will be holding their own debate from the perspective of either the ulamas or the Mutazilites. Divide the class into two sections, one to represent each of these groups. Students can use the information in the chapter as well as do other research to organize an argument on the issue of whether or not people control their ultimate destiny. The culminating activity could be a class debate on the issue in which a representative from each group can present his or her group's ideas, and then each group can take questions from the other group to clarify any points or give more information. Share with the class the assessment rubric in the back of this guide.

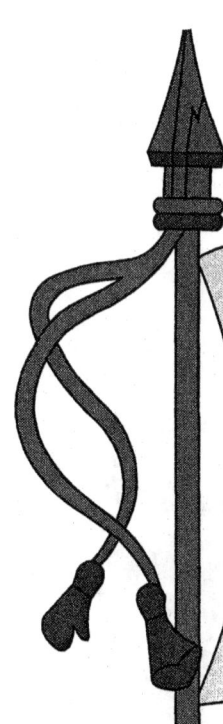

Chapter 7
▸ Arts and Sciences Museum Tours

The Islamic Empire became the center of thought for the sciences and the arts. Students can work in pairs to research three artistic or scientific developments in the Islamic Empire and prepare a presentation for each development as it would be made by a museum tour guide. Students should collect as many visual items as they can about the developments they research and display them in an organized fashion on a wall in the classroom. This project could culminate with the pairs acting as tour guides for the class and directing them through their visual aids and explaining the significance of each display. Share with the class the assessment rubric in the back of this guide.

Chapter 8
▸ Illustrated Essay

Divide the class into small groups to create an illustrated essay of the chapter. The essays should include up to ten panels of illustrations, each of which represents an important event or person discussed in the chapter. The panels should be visual representations with short captions, if necessary, to describe the actions in the illustrations. Students can think of these panels as a way of summarizing the text for someone who has not read the chapter. Before making their illustrations, groups should agree upon which events are the most important and then assign artists to each event. This project could culminate with a presentation of the panels in sequential order by each group. Share with the class the assessment rubric in the back of this guide.

Chapter 9
▸ Extreme Makeover—The Life of the Ghana

The Ghana was considered a divine king who had sacred powers. This person inherited the position from his mother's brother. Have partners research what life was like for the Ghana and write a set of three to five journal entries describing the steps in becoming the Ghana. Students should consider the personal reflections of this person as he transforms from a regular person to a divine king, taking on the many new responsibilities and expectations. This project could culminate with the students using their word-processing skills to publish their Ghana journals and then share their journals with the class. Share with the class the assessment rubric in the back of this guide.

Chapter 10
▸ Pen Pals from Across the Empire

Divide the class into partners. Ask the partners to decide which of them is from Mali and which is from Songhay. Have students review the chapter, taking notes in their history journals about the characteristics of the place they are representing. Then have students write letters to each other as if they are from Mali or Songhay, describing the features of their area and what life is like for them. Partners can practice their word-processing skills to write at least three letters to each other. They can include questions for their pen pal about life in Mali or Songhay, which the person may have to do further research to answer. This project could culminate with oral presentations of the written dialogue between the pen pals. Share with the class the assessment rubric in the back of this guide.

Chapter 11
▸ Life in Bronze

The Obas had bronze and brass castings made of themselves to represent their lives and their kingships. Other court officials had their likenesses cast in bronze as well. Have students reread the last three paragraphs of the chapter. Provide time for students to use this information to think about how they would represent their own lives in a bronze casting, and which symbols they would use to symbolize their skills and characteristics. For homework, students can sketch their casting and make notes of the details that they wish to include on it. Then provide time in class for students to create a three-dimensional image using clay or other materials. Point out that they will be creating a sculpture and not a casting, which is a method of carving out a form, pouring liquid such as melted brass or bronze into it, and then letting it cool before removing it from the mold. Share with the class the assessment rubric in the back of this guide.

Chapter 12
▶ Digging for Facts

Most of what is known about Mapungubwe and Great Zimbabwe has been collected by archaeologists from the remains of the civilization and the city. Divide the class into small groups and have them review the information on pages 138-144 about these cities and what archaeologists believe to be true about life there. Then have the small groups make a list of five to ten items that they use everyday. Ask students to imagine they are archaeologists 800 years from now who discover these objects. Have students record what they think the items might be used for and what the items say about the civilization that used them. Point out that some of the archaeologists' ideas about Mapungubwe and Great Zimbabwe can apply to items that students choose from today. For example, if students choose a pencil, an archaeologist in 800 years might remark that it is made from wood that is not indigenous to the location it was found, making it likely that it was imported from a different area and point to trade with other areas as a way of life in this civilization. Each small group can present their findings about the items chosen to the class. Share with the class the assessment rubric in the back of this guide.

Chapter 13
▶ A Day in the Life on the Swahili Coast

The chapter tells about what life was like for a girl and a boy on the Swahili coast in 1498. Explain that students are going to compare the lives of Swahili boys and girls in 1498 and today. Have students work in pairs to reread pages 150-155 and take notes in their history journals, organizing the information on a two-column chart with the headings *Swahili girls* and *Swahili boys*. To further organize the information, students can give each item on the list a symbol to represent the type of information it is (for example, education, chores, and religious life). For homework, students can research what life is like for boys and girls on the Swahili coast today. Their research may be easier if they choose one particular city to study. Also, pairs may choose to split up the research with one student researching girls and the other boys. Students can look for information to compare to the information given in the text, or even do further research on the lives of boys and girls on the Swahili coast in 1498. Allow class time for partners to compare what they have discovered and organize their information onto a chart. They may wish to use a Venn diagram or another graphic organizer. This project could culminate with presentations by each pair of students. Share with the class the assessment rubric in the back of this guide. As each pair presents, the other students may want to rate their performance against the rubric.

CHAPTER 1
CAMELS, CARAVANS, AND THE KA'BA: THE ARABIAN PENINSULA AROUND 600 (PAGES 15–23)

FOR HOMEWORK

STUDENT STUDY GUIDE
pages 11–14

CHAPTER SUMMARY

By the end of the 6th century, the trading town of Mecca had been a place where traders from the East and West had been meeting to exchange goods for hundreds of years. Trade was dangerous because of conflicts regarding land, as well as attacks by the Bedouin: a nomadic, polytheistic, and democratic group who live in the desert.

PERFORMANCE OBJECTIVES

- To understand the importance of trade and trade routes in 6th-century Arabia
- To explain how the Bedouin lived in the Arabian Desert
- To identify the characteristics of different groups of people living in 6th-century Arabia
- To provide background for understanding the surroundings in which Muhammad, the prophet of Islam, was born and reared

BUILDING BACKGROUND

Ask students to name some of the items they buy at malls or at grocery stores. Have them describe how these products might get from where they are made or grown to these shopping centers. For example: explain how bananas are grown in South America, picked, and shipped by trucks, trains, and planes before they reach a grocery store in the United States. Then ask students what they think it would be like to have to make a dangerous journey over hundreds of miles without the help of trucks, trains, planes, or freighter ships in order to supply the things their community needs. Explain that this chapter is about how trade took place in the 6th century in Arabia.

VOCABULARY

caravan a group of people, animals, and vehicles traveling together through the desert

trade the exchange of goods

nomads people who do not settle in one place but move from place to place based on weather and seasons

polytheistic believing in more than one god

Students can also consult the glossary to define the following words:
Allah, Bedouin, Byzantine, clan, Ka'ba, Quraysh, rainforest, Ramadan, Sassanid, shaykh, tribe.

CHAPTER 1

WORKING WITH PRIMARY SOURCES

The sidebar on Student Edition page 17 contains a quote written by the historian Procopius that refers to the barren nature of the northern section of the Arabian Peninsula. In small groups, have students read the quote and illustrate the desolate scene it describes. Then ask students to point out specific words that Procopius used that inspired their groups' drawings.

GEOGRAPHY CONNECTION

Movement Have students look at a physical or topographic map that includes the Middle East, Europe, and Asia. Have them locate Mecca on the map and trace the routes that may have been followed by the traders in the chapter. Point out that some of the places mentioned in the chapter now have different names. For example, Constantinople is now Istanbul, Turkey. Have students discuss what challenges they think the traders might have faced because of the characteristics of the land they traveled over.

READING COMPREHENSION QUESTIONS

1. Why was the Ka'ba important to the Arabs of the 6th century? (*It was considered a sacred building where sacred idols and stones were kept.*)
2. Why was it dangerous for a caravan trader to travel the route north of Mecca? (*This route ran through areas of war and conflict over access to water. Also, the Bedouin often attacked and robbed the caravans in this area.*)
3. Why were the Bedouin tribes nomadic and how did this affect their daily lives? (*They did not farm because of the lack of rain in the areas where they lived, so they had to continually move from place to place looking for water for themselves and pastureland for their herds.*)
4. What led to the increase in trade in Mecca during Ramadan? (*The Quraysh tribe convinced the Bedouin not to attack during the holy month of Ramadan, ensuring the safe passage of traders in and out of the city.*)

CRITICAL THINKING QUESTIONS

1. What do you think made Mecca a good center for trade? (*Possible answers: Mecca was centrally located between trading countries of the East and West. Its location was accessible to traders coming by land or sea. It also was an oasis.*)
2. How do you think the nomadic nature of the Bedouin affected their culture? (*Possible answers: They had a lot of reverence for their camels due to their dependence on the camel for continuous moving; they were not overly materialistic as a culture since they were only able to possess what they could transport.*)
3. Do you suppose that stopping the Bedouin attacks for the month of Ramadan would have increased or decreased trade over all? (*Possible answers: It would have increased trade because more people would have come at one time to do more trading; it would have decreased trade because traders might have only come during that one month of the year and not trade the rest of the year.*)

SOCIAL SCIENCES

Civics The government of the United States is a democracy. Ask students to compare and contrast the way the United States government is run with the way that the democratic Bedouin tribes were organized.

THEN and NOW

In the 6th and 7th centuries, the Bedouin lived mostly in Arabia. The Bedouin of today live throughout the Middle East and northern Africa but have managed to maintain some of the same traditions, though many Bedouin are exchanging their nomadic lifestyles for a settled life in urban areas. There are numerous websites about the Bedouin people of today and the fragility of their culture. For example, visit www.geographia.com/egypt/sinai/bedouin02.htm, www.worldpress.org/Mideast/1978.cfm or i-cias.com/e.0/bedouins.htm.

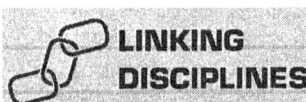

LINKING DISCIPLINES

Science Conditions such as weather and climate made traveling in the desert dangerous for traders. Ask students to find information about the temperatures and conditions during the different seasons in the Arabian Desert. Have them suggest when they think would be the best time for traders to travel.

AFRICAN & MIDDLE EASTERN WORLD, 600–1500

LITERATURE CONNECTION

Cornell University Library's Middle East & Islamic Studies website has some general information about Middle Eastern and Islamic literature. This website gives information and provides links with more details about the rich heritage of literature from this region of the world: www.library.cornell.edu/colldev/mideast. "Arab Gateway" website offers information on and samples of classic Arabic poetry, in addition to related links and resources: www.al-bab.com/arab/literature/poetry.htm. Also, Lila Abu-Lughod's *Writing Women's Worlds: Bedouin Stories* (Berkeley: University of California Press, 1993), is an interesting collection of stories from the Nomadic pastoral people of the Arabian desert.

LITERACY TIPS

In addition to using the suggestions in the Supporting Learning and Extending Learning sections, refer back frequently to pages 16–19 for strategies and advice from a literacy coach.

READING AND LANGUAGE ARTS

Reading Nonfiction Read the first paragraph of the chapter aloud. Ask students to answer the question words *who, what, when, where, why,* and *how,* using details from the paragraph.

Using Language Students can find examples of first-, second-, and third-person writing in the chapter. Encourage them to look at all features and sidebars. Explain that first-person writing uses *I, we, me,* or *us;* second-person writing uses *you* or *your;* and third-person writing uses *he, she, him, her, it, they,* or *them.* Ask students to identify examples in Chapter 1 of each of these three perspectives or points of view.

WRITING

Persuasion The Quraysh tribe convinced the Bedouin to break from attacking caravan groups during the month of Ramadan because it was a holy month. Write a letter persuading the Bedouin to not attack traders for a second month each year.

SUPPORTING LEARNING

English Language Learners Have partners make a list of nouns in the chapter, such as statues, spices, caravan, and desert. Partners should then give an example of how each noun can be used and how is it is related to the main ideas in the chapter. For example, students might tell how the desert affected life on the Arabian Peninsula.

Struggling Readers Ask students to use the main idea map (see reproducibles at the back of this guide) to show the experiences of a caravan guide in 6th century Arabia. Have students write *Life of a caravan guide* in the center and surround it with details about a caravan guide's life.

EXTENDING LEARNING

Enrichment Pairs of students can research the meaning of Ramadan today and compare it to the description of the month of Ramadan in the chapter.

Extension Have students look at the image of the Ka'ba on page 34 (Chapter 2) and read the caption. Then have them reread the second paragraph of the first chapter and compare and contrast the written description of the Ka'ba of the 6th century with the visual image depicting the Ka'ba.

CHAPTER 1

NAME   **DATE**

CAMELS, CARAVANS, AND THE KA'BA: THE ARABIAN PENINSULA AROUND 600

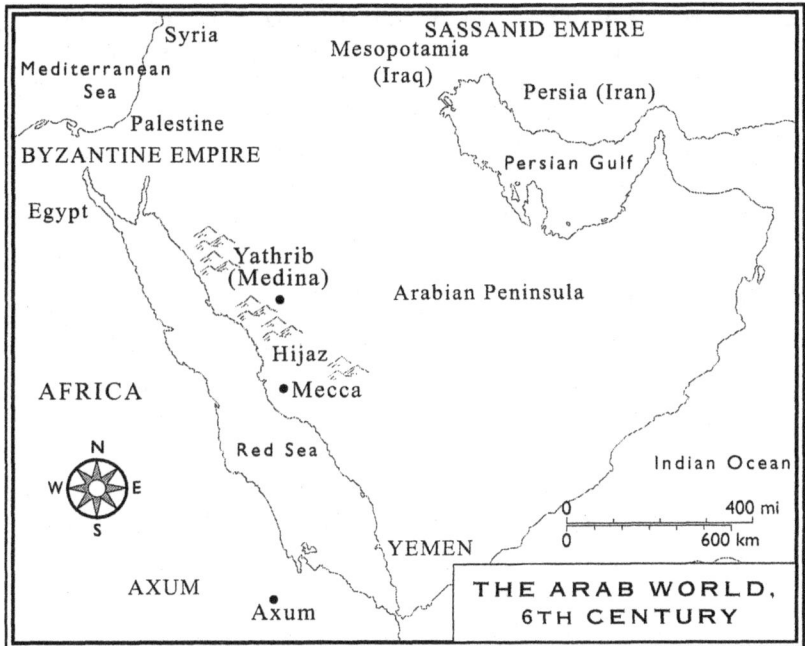

Directions

Study the map showing the Arab world in the 6th century. Use information from the chapter to follow the directions given below.

1. Draw a symbol on the map showing the location of the Ka'ba. Add this symbol to the map legend and label it Ka'ba.
   _____
   _____

2. Where does wheat grow? Draw a symbol for wheat on the map. Add the symbol and label for wheat to the map legend.
   _____
   _____

3. Shade in the dangerous area of the map where people are fighting over the better-watered areas. Add a box with the shading to the map legend and label the symbol "dangerous area."
   _____
   _____

CHAPTER 1 BLM   AFRICAN & MIDDLE EASTERN WORLD, 600–1500   **29**

NAME   **DATE**

PRIMARY SOURCES

Directions

The poem excerpt below is from Student Edition page 21. The poem, by Imru-Ul-Quais, was written on the wall of the Ka'ba at some point before 622. Read the excerpt and then answer the questions below.

> "Then I said, 'Drive him on! Let his reins go loose, while you turn to me.
> Think not of the camel and our weight on him. Let us be happy.'"

1. How do these lines reflect the nomadic nature of the Bedouin?

2. How does the placement of this poem on the walls of the Ka'ba shade the meaning of the poem?

3. How does the narrator of this poem create a commanding presence through his words?

4. Extend this poem by writing the next few lines as if you are responding to the narrator's command.

NAME **DATE**

CHAPTER TEST 1
THE AFRICAN & MIDDLE EASTERN WORLD, 600–1500

A. MULTIPLE CHOICE

Circle the letter of the best answer to each question.

1. The Ka'ba was an important place for Arabs because
   a. it was a sacred building that housed statues and stones.
   b. it was as tall as a man.
   c. the courtyard around it was full of idols.
   d. it was located in the square in Mecca.

2. Why did a caravan guide go to Yemen's ports?
   a. The ports were on the way to Mecca.
   b. He went to meet traders who had luxury goods from around the Indian Ocean.
   c. They were exciting places to visit.
   d. They got regular rainfall.

3. Why were people fighting over the land north of Mecca?
   a. The Bedouin people lived there.
   b. The bandits and robbers ran rampant.
   c. The Byzantine and Sassanid empires were becoming weak.
   d. There was more rainfall there than in other places, making the pastureland good.

4. The Bedouin were called a democracy because
   a. they were a nomadic people.
   b. they never let one person get too much power.
   c. they liked to speak their minds.
   d. women were rarely allowed to participate in decision-making.

5. The Bedouin allowed safe passage of caravans in and out of Mecca during Ramadan because
   a. there were so many sacred idols at the shrine in Mecca.
   b. it would increase trade.
   c. Ramadan was a holy month.
   d. they are a polytheistic people.

B. SHORT ANSWER

Write one or two sentences to answer each question.

6. How did the Quraysh tribe arrange for Ramadan to take place?

   _____

   _____

7. How would you describe the range of religions in 6th century Arabia?

   _____

   _____

C. ESSAY

In an essay, explain how Bedouin society was organized in 6th-century Arabia. What were the reasons for this system of organization? Support your essay with details from the chapter.

CHAPTER 2: THE MESSENGER OF ALLAH: MUHAMMAD AND THE BEGINNING OF ISLAM (PAGES 24–34)

FOR HOMEWORK
STUDENT STUDY GUIDE
pages 15–18

CAST OF CHARACTERS

Muhammad (moo-HAH-mud) **ibn Abdallah** (ub-duh-LAH) **al-Hashimi** (al-hah-SHEE-mee) founder of the Islamic religion, considered God's last and greatest prophet by his followers; united many Arab tribes and converted them to worshipping one God

Abu (uh-BOO) **Talib** (TAH-lib) Muhammad's uncle, who raised Muhammad when he became an orphan

Khadija (hah-DEE-jah) a wealthy widow, she was Muhammad's first wife and his first convert to Islam

CHAPTER SUMMARY

The prophet Muhammad was the founder of the Muslim religion. Though at first many rejected his message and teachings, he later converted many people of Arabia, including the Quraysh tribe of his birth city, Mecca. The Muslim people practiced the Five Pillars of Islam as well as followed other rules.

PERFORMANCE OBJECTIVES

▶ To understand the life and teachings of the prophet Muhammad
▶ To explain the role of the prophet Muhammad as the founder of Islam
▶ To summarize the events leading to the rise of Islam in the Middle East
▶ To understand the new kind of society Muhammad established in Medina.

BUILDING BACKGROUND

Elicit details from students about early Islam. Have them tell what they know about who founded it, where it began, and what the teachings were.

VOCABULARY

prophet one who tells the word of God
merchant a trader or one who runs a business
meditation spending quiet time deep in thought
revelation a truth which God makes known
convert to change to another's way of thinking or believing
arbitration to listen to both sides of an argument and make a decision
pilgrimage a journey to a sacred place

As needed, have students consult the glossary to define the following words: *Arabic, Five Pillars of Islam, hijra, Islam, Muslims, Quran, Umma.*

WORKING WITH PRIMARY SOURCES

Help students understand that one of the sources used in the chapter is the Quran, which is the holy book of Islam. This book was written specifically for followers of that religion. The other sources were written by historians. Have students infer how the religious text differs from the history texts.

GEOGRAPHY CONNECTION

Location Have students locate Axum and Yemen on a map. Ask volunteers to suggest possibilities for how the Axumites might have traveled to invade Yemen in 525.

READING COMPREHENSION QUESTIONS

1. Why did the Axumites invade Yemen? (*The Yemeni king was persecuting Christians in Axum and so the Axumites, who were Christians, took revenge on the king.*)
2. Why was the "Year of the Elephant" important? (*It was the year the Axumites attacked Mecca and the year the Prophet Muhammad was born.*)
3. What happened to Muhammad that made him realize that he was to become a prophet? (*Muslims believe he was visited by Gabriel, an angel of God, who told him to teach people about what God wanted.*)
4. What did Muhammad do while he was teaching in Mecca? (*He settled disputes between tribes; he established a community based on shared beliefs.*)
5. Why was the Black Stone in the Ka'ba important to the Muslims? (*They believed the stone had been given to Abraham, the father of the Jewish, Christian, and Muslim religions, for the building of a shrine.*)

CRITICAL THINKING QUESTIONS

1. When Muhmmad first began to preach, which of God's messages worried his fellow Meccans and why? (*the belief that there was only one God, and the threat this posed for their religious shrine*)
2. What might Muhammad's ability to settle the disputes of people from different religious groups say about his character? (*Possible answer: He was open-minded and did not judge people based on their beliefs of backgrounds.*)
3. What do you think Muhammad was thinking when he smashed all of the images and idols in the Ka'ba? (*Possible answer: He was angry that the idols were there because they represented beliefs in many gods but he believed in only one God.*)

SOCIAL SCIENCES

Religion and Society The Quran required that each Muslim travel to Mecca at least once in a lifetime. Have students in pairs research how Muslims of today, who live all over the world, make this pilgrimage. Have each pair choose a different place in the world where Muslims live, then have them research and map how believers from that part of the world might reach Mecca.

READING AND LANGUAGE ARTS

Reading Nonfiction Elicit from students that the type of information that is given in the chapter about Muhammad is called biographical information. Have students briefly review the chapter and offer some points of biographical information about Muhammad.

Using Language Ask students to carefully read the quote describing the rewards that will be offered when Judgment comes in the last paragraph on page 26. Point out the ellipsis. Explain that writers use this symbol (…) to indicate where some words have been left out of the actual quotation.

THEN and NOW

Early Muslims only lived in Arabia and areas close to Mecca. Today, only about 20 percent of Muslims come from this area and there are more than 1.2 billion followers of Islam living all over the world. Presently, the majority of the world's Muslims live in Asian countries.

LINKING DISCIPLINES

Art Though the Quran forbade representing people in art because it might lead to idol worship, many everyday items were elaborately decorated with patterns and images. To see some examples of early Islamic art, visit the Los Angeles County Museum of Art website at *www.lacma.org/islamic_art/eia.htm*. Have students choose one work and draw or create something of their own that uses the same images or patterns in some way. Ask student what they think those images or patterns indicate or mean, and why?

LITERACY TIPS

In addition to using the suggestions in the Supporting Learning and Extending Learning sections, refer back frequently to pages 16–19 for strategies and advice from a literacy coach.

WRITING

News article Have students pretend they are reporters for the town of Yathrib who are writing about the invitation the town has extended Muhammad and his followers to come settle there. Reporters might tell the story as if Muhammad has just been asked, or after he arrives and the town becomes, under Muhammad's direction, Medina. Tell them to be sure to include the "who, what, where, when, why, and how" of the situation.

SUPPORTING LEARNING

English Language Learners Have students use a dictionary to learn the meaning of the word pillar. Have them relate the dictionary meaning (a support for a structure or building) to the way it is used in "The Five Pillars of Islam." Then have students talk about other ways in which words related to building and homes are used metaphorically. For example, can they find two ways to use words like *foundation, window,* or *door*?

Struggling Readers Ask students to use the outline graphic organizer (see reproducibles at the back of this guide) to organize the main ideas and details related to Muhammad's life.

EXTENDING LEARNING

Enrichment Have students use the Internet and articles and books to find out how Muslims of today uphold the "Five Pillars of Islam" in their lives. Some useful websites are *www.islamicity.com/mosque/pillars.shtml* and *www.islamic-paths.org/Home/English/Discover/Pillars_Main.htm*.

Extension Ask students to research the historical events of Muhammad's life. Then ask them to create a timeline of these events. They can use the timeline graphic organizer (see reproducibles at the back of this guide) to organize their information. Have them identify which events seem most significant, then illustrate one of them to add to the timeline.

NAME   **DATE**

MESSENGER OF ALLAH

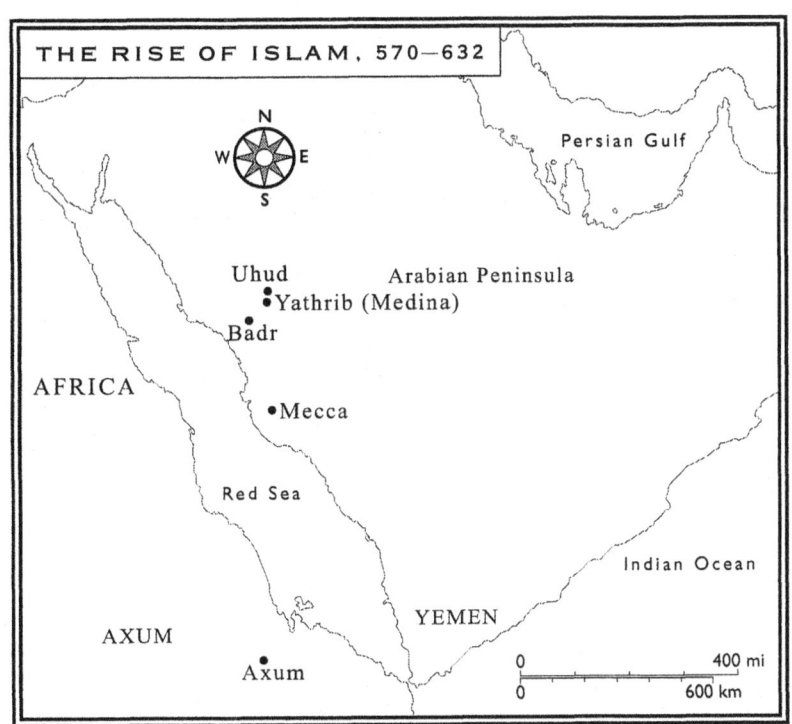

Directions

Study the map of the Arabian Peninsula. Use this map and information from the chapter to answer the questions that follow.

1. Use arrows to show the movement of the Axumites through Yemen and on toward Mecca. In which directions did the Axumites travel?

2. Mecca is closest to which body of water?

3. Circle the town where Muhammad's followers ambushed a caravan in 624.

4. Draw an "x" at the town where the Battle of the Ditch took place.

5. Underline the name of the place where the Black Stone can be found.

CHAPTER 2 BLM   AFRICAN & MIDDLE EASTERN WORLD, 600–1500   **35**

PRIMARY SOURCES

Directions

Read the passage below. Then answer the questions that follow.

> When God sent his Prophet, who came preaching the unity of God and calling for His worship alone without any associate, [the Arabs] said, "maketh he the god to be but one god? A strange thing forsooth is this." They had in mind the idols [they had previously worshipped].

1. Summarize in your own words what this passage says.

2. How do you think the Arabs felt when they heard Muhammad's preaching? Why?

3. What is the difference between polytheism and monotheism? How does this text show a clash between the two?

CHAPTER TEST 2

THE AFRICAN & MIDDLE EASTERN WORLD, 600–1500

NAME _____ DATE _____

A. MULTIPLE CHOICE

Circle the letter of the best answer to each question.

1. The "Year of the Elephant" was important because
    a. it was when Muhammad married Khadija.
    b. it was the year Muhammad was born.
    c. it was when Muhammad made a pilgrimage to Mecca.
    d. it was the year Muhammad died.

2. What happened when Muhammad was 40 years old?
    a. He was visited by an angel of God.
    b. He destroyed the idols in the Ka'ba.
    c. He became the great leader of the Muslim people.
    d. He led his followers to war.

3. The messages that God gave to Muhammad all of the following themes **except**
    a. there is only one God.
    b. there will be a Day of Judgment.
    c. judgment will occur on earth.
    d. people should cease worshipping idols.

4. Muhammad preached that the welfare of these people, in particular, was of utmost importance to God.
    a. the rich
    b. those who worship idols
    c. the poor and slaves
    d. children

5. Medina was an entirely new kind of society for Arabia because
    a. it was based on Muslim law.
    b. it was based on the idea of one, true God.
    c. it was a democratic government.
    d. tribes fought each other for supremacy.

6. The "Five Pillars of Islam" are important because they
    a. tell people not to eat pork or drink alcohol.
    b. explain how to get to Mecca.
    c. tell the basic duties of every Muslim.
    d. tell the story of Muhammad's life.

B. SHORT ANSWER

Write one or two sentences to answer each question.

7. How did Muhammad first become a prophet, and how did he first begin his preaching?

_____
_____
_____

8. What are the "Five Pillars of Islam"?

_____
_____
_____

C. ESSAY

Summarize the life of Muhammad and early Islam by writing an essay in which you sequence at least four key moments as described in Chapter 2 of the Student Edition.

THE SWORD OF ALLAH: THE ISLAMIC EXPANSION, 632-750
(PAGES 35-44)

FOR HOMEWORK

STUDENT STUDY GUIDE
pages 19-22

CHAPTER SUMMARY

After the death of Muhammad, Abu Bakr led the Muslims, under whose two-year leadership Islam spread all over the Arabian Peninsula. Umar then led the Muslims to expand Islam throughout northern Africa, converting many Berbers, including Tariq, a general who led the Muslim conquest into Europe.

PERFORMANCE OBJECTIVES

► To understand the succession of leadership in the Muslim religion after Muhammad
► To describe the expansion of Islamic rule through northern Africa to Europe
► To summarize some of the key events that assisted in the spread of Islam
► To compare and contrast the Berber and Bedouin cultures

BUILDING BACKGROUND

Initiate a discussion about inheritance. Ask students to tell stories of how things are passed on after someone dies. Explain that this chapter tells how the leadership of the Muslim religion was passed on after Muhammad died.

VOCABULARY

heir a person who receives property or position after the death of the owner
deputy a person who is second in command or an assistant
alliance a connection or friendship between families or political groups
resisters those who fight against something

As needed, have students consult the glossary to define the following words: *Andalusian, Berbers, caliphs, jihad, oral tradition, Sanhaja, shaykh, Tuareg.*

WORKING WITH PRIMARY SOURCES

The Berbers were known for their incredible survival skills. Have students read the 1st-century geographer Strabo's descriptions of the Berbers on Student Edition pages 41-42. After they have read these descriptions, have them create word webs to display those words that portray the Berbers as "survivors."

CAST OF CHARACTERS

Abu (uh-BOO) **Bakr** (BACK-er) Muhammad's closest friend and the first male convert to Islam who became first caliph

Umar (oo-MAHR) second caliph

Tariq (TAR-ehk) Muslim general

GEOGRAPHY CONNECTION

Movement Have students look at the map on page 37 and trace the path that the Muslim groups followed as they spread Islam. Discuss with students how the Islamic areas differ during this time from the time of Muhammad.

READING COMPREHENSION QUESTIONS

1. How did the Muslim community respond after Muhammad's death? *(They voted on a person to become the new leader and chose Abu Bakr.)*
2. What did Abu Bakr accomplish while he was the leader of the Muslims? *(He brought people back to Islam and helped to spread Islam across the entire Arabian Peninsula.)*
3. What did the Muslims believe would happen to a person who died while fighting in a legal war? *(The person would be guaranteed a place in heaven on the Day of Judgment.)*
4. What was Umar's mission? *(He wanted to spread Islamic rule beyond the borders of the Arabian Peninsula.)*
5. How did Islamic rule spread in Spain? *(The Berber general, Tariq, led his army across the Mediterranean Sea from Morocco into Spain where, after a few years, he and his men took over much of the Spanish peninsula.)*

CRITICAL THINKING QUESTIONS

1. Read what Abu Bakr said when he accepted his position as leader of the Muslims. What do you think these words say about Abu Bakr's character? *(He was a humble man who trusted his fellow Muslims to help him do his job well.)*
2. Why do you think the Muslims were able to advance into Spain but not into Constantinople? *(Possible answer: A high wall surrounded Constantinople and the Byzantines had a weapon called "Greek fire." This shows that they were strong warriors and prepared to fight the Muslims. The Spanish were divided and perhaps unprepared for the attack, and as well, the Muslims were being led by Tariq, a strong leader who was able to rally his men.)*
3. How might Muslims have benefited from the treaty with non-Muslim groups asking these groups to live peacefully with them? *(Possible answer: The Muslims would be assured that no other groups would attack them. Also, these non-Muslims would become sources of tax monies needed to support the Muslims.)*

SOCIAL SCIENCES

Economics Under the leadership of Abu Bakr, the Muslim community was prospering and therefore attracted many new followers who wanted to share in the wealth. Encourage students to find out what the economy of the Muslims of this time was based on and what economic factors created such prosperity. Students can display their findings in charts.

READING AND LANGUAGE ARTS

Reading Nonfiction Ask students to draw a timeline of the Islamic expansion as presented in the chapter. Then have them summarize the events in their own words using time-order words such as next, then, after, etc.

Using Language Have students make a list of the characters in the chapter. Then ask them to write two or three adjectives to describe each person. Remind students that adjectives are words that describe nouns. Examples of adjectives include words such as *strong*, *tall*, and *funny*.

THEN and NOW

Although the original Berbers were known to be nomads, most contemporary Berbers can be found settled in Morocco and Algeria. Today they prefer the name Amazigh to the title Berber.

LINKING DISCIPLINES

Science The chapter mentions that the weather conditions in the Sahara Desert are still as harsh as they were during the mid-7th century. Have students research past and present weather conditions in the Sahara Desert: temperature, yearly rainfall, seasonal change, etc. Students can then make a chart or graph showing these changes over time.

LITERACY TIPS

In addition to using the suggestions in the Supporting Learning and Extending Learning sections, refer back frequently to pages 16-19 for strategies and advice from a literacy coach.

WRITING

News Article Have students write news articles as if they were wartime correspondents who were present during the warfare that took place between the Byzantines and the Arab armies under Umar. Students should review Student Edition pages 38-40 to learn more about the course of the wars, and they can supplement this material with additional research for homework (via the Internet or the local library). After students have completed their research, have them write a news article on the battles. Reportage should be done as if from the scene of the event and include interviews with hypothetical or historic witnesses or participants. This project could culminate with the class creating a mock broadcast covering the warfare for an ancient audience.

EXTENDING LEARNING

Enrichment In the chapter, the Berber people of North Africa are compared with the Bedouin of the Arabian Peninsula. Have students do research to learn more about the Berber people. Divide students into small groups and have them make Venn diagrams comparing and contrasting what they learned about the Berber people with what they know about the Bedouin. Groups can use their completed Venn diagrams as visual aids as they orally present their conclusions.

Extension Ask students to work in pairs to review the chapter and create a timeline of events during the Islamic expansion. Have them use a timeline chart (see reproducibles at the back of this guide) to organize the information.

SUPPORTING LEARNING

English Language Learners Ask students to find examples of adverbs and adjectives in the chapter. Have them write down five examples of each and use each one in a sentence. Then have students explain how each adverb or adjective helps to make the ideas in the chapter clearer. Review with students that adverbs are words that describe verbs, or action words, and adjectives are words that describe nouns.

Struggling Readers Have students create sequence diagrams showing the order of events in the spread of Islam. They may choose to begin their diagram with "Muhammad dies and Abu Bakr becomes leader of the Muslims."

NAME   **DATE**

THE ISLAMIC EXPANSION

Directions

Study the map, which shows Islamic areas in 749. Then answer the questions.

1. Use the mileage scale to figure out the approximate distance that Islam spread both east and west of Medina.
   _____
   _____
   _____

2. Use a colored pencil to color in the areas where Islam spread under Abu Bakr's leadership.
   _____
   _____
   _____
   _____

3. Use a different color to show those areas where Islam spread under Umar's leadership.
   _____
   _____
   _____

4. The text says that the Muslims were not able to advance into Constantinople in the Byzantine Empire. What geographical features may have also helped to limit their expansion northward?
   _____
   _____
   _____

CHAPTER 3 BLM   AFRICAN & MIDDLE EASTERN WORLD, 600–1500   **41**

PRIMARY SOURCES

Directions

Read the quote from the Berber general Tariq below. Then answer the questions that follow.

> Oh my warriors. . . . Behind you is the sea, before you, the enemy. You have left now only the hope of your courage and your constancy. . . . Remember that if you suffer a few moments in patience, you will afterward enjoy supreme delight. Do not imagine that your fate can be separated from mine, and rest assured that if you fall, I shall perish with you, or avenge you . . . The Commander of True Believers . . . has chosen you for this attack from among all his Arab warriors. . . . the one fruit which he desires to obtain from your bravery is that the word of God shall be exalted in the country, and that the true religion shall be established here. The spoils will belong to yourselves.

1. To whom is Tariq speaking?

2. How does Tariq say that he is connected with the people to whom he is speaking?

3. Who is "The Commander of True Believers" to whom Tariq is referring?

4. What does Tariq think that this "Commander of True Believers" wants?

CHAPTER TEST 3

THE AFRICAN & MIDDLE EASTERN WORLD, 600–1500

NAME   **DATE**

A. MULTIPLE CHOICE

Circle the letter of the best answer to each question.

1. Who was the Islamic leader after Muhammad?
   - a. Ali
   - b. Umar
   - c. Tariq
   - d. Abu Bakr

2. Under Abu Bakr's leadership, Islam was spread
   - a. into the Berber tribes.
   - b. into Spain.
   - c. throughout the Arabian Peninsula.
   - d. across northern Africa.

3. Under Umar, the Muslims were not successful spreading Islam into
   - a. Spain.
   - b. northern Africa.
   - c. Constantinople.
   - d. Egypt.

4. The Berbers were
   - a. nomads of northern Africa.
   - b. Arab warriors.
   - c. converted to Islam by Abu Bakr.
   - d. from Mecca.

5. Tariq was
   - a. the son-in-law and cousin of Muhammad.
   - b. an Islamic prophet.
   - c. a Berber general.
   - d. an Islamic caliph.

B. SHORT ANSWER

Write one or two sentences to answer each question.

6. How does the spread of Islamic rule relate to their religious beliefs?

_____
_____
_____

7. How did Umar use military strategy to attack the Byzantines and Sassanids?

_____
_____
_____

C. ESSAY

In an essay, compare and contrast the Berber and Bedouin cultures. How were the two cultures similar? How did their cultures differ? How did they eventually influence one another? Support your essay with details from the chapter.

CHAPTER 4

MANAGING THE EMPIRE: ISLAM GROWS INTO AN EMPIRE OF FAITH (PAGES 45–54)

FOR HOMEWORK

STUDENT STUDY GUIDE pages 23–26

CHAPTER SUMMARY

After the Muslim leader Umar was killed, controversy regarding the rightful leadership of Islam became heated. Uthman succeeded Umar, followed by Ali and then Muawiyah, leading to about 90 years of leadership by the Umayyads. Throughout this time, factions began to develop within the Muslim communities.

PERFORMANCE OBJECTIVES

- To identify the Muslim leaders after Umar
- To explain how these leaders came to power
- To describe the various groups of believers and their interactions with one another

BUILDING BACKGROUND

Ask students what they know about the democratic process for finding leaders in the United States and how the different political parties interact with one another. Explain that the chapter they are about to read is about how the leadership of Islam was decided upon and how different groups of Muslims reacted to these decisions.

VOCABULARY

zakat a charitable tax paid by Muslims

jizya a special tax paid by non-Muslims

faction a party or group within a governing body which disagrees with those who govern

pillaging taking goods and killing without mercy

assassination the killing of a famous person

diplomacy handling relations between groups in a peaceful way

As needed, have students consult the glossary to define the following words: *imam, Kharijites, mawalis, Shiite, Sunnis, Umayyad, zakat.*

WORKING WITH PRIMARY SOURCES

The Sunnah is the second source of Islamic law after the Quran. The Quran is considered by Muslims as the only authentic revelation of Allah to humanity. The Quran, taken as the word of Allah incorporated in the book called Mus-haf, and the Sunna, incorporated in many books (the most important of which are Sahih Bukhari, Sahih Muslim, Sunan An-Nasai, Sunan Attirmidhi, Sunan Ibn Majah, and Sunan Abu Daud), are considered divine directives for Muslims worldwide.

The Quran is the holiest book for all Muslims around the world. The Sunna tells how the prophet Muhammad lived his life and is the second source of Islamic law after the Quran. The Quran has been translated into many languages. At the website *www.quran-islam.org/183.html*, it can be read in 22 different translations.

CAST OF CHARACTERS

Uthman (OOTH-mahn) third caliph

Ali (AH-lee) fourth caliph, assassinated by a Kharijite fanatic

Muawiyah (moo-AH-wee-yah) fifth caliph and founder of the Umayyad dynasty

GEOGRAPHY CONNECTION

Location Have students review the chapter, taking note of how the center of the Muslim religion was moved from place to place by the different leaders. Ask students to look at a map of the region and point out the various places that were at one time the center for the Muslims (Mecca, Medina, and Damascus)

READING COMPREHENSION QUESTIONS

1. What led to the death of Umar? (*Taxes were imposed upon non-Muslims, and one slave who was unable to get relief from the tax killed Umar out of anger.*)
2. How did Uthman become the next Islamic leader? How did people react to his appointment as leader? (*People chose him because he came from the Umayyad clan and was a good manager. Some people did not like him because the Umayyads had been Muhammad's opponents and they wanted Ali to be the next leader.*)
3. What important contribution did Uthman make to Islam before his death? (*He had all the messages God sent Muhammad collected and written down in one book. This became the official version of the Quran.*)
4. Why did Uthman's cousin, Muawiyah, oppose the appointment of Ali as the Islamic leader after Uthman's death? (*He believed he should be the next caliph because he was Uthman's cousin and the governor of Syria. He also believed Ali had not shown enough interest in bringing the murders of Uthman to justice.*)
5. Who were the mawalis and why were they angry? (*The mawalis were non-Arab Muslims. They were angry because they were forced to pay the non-Muslim tax (jizya) and were treated as a lower class.*)

CRITICAL THINKING QUESTIONS

1. What does the fact that Muslim conquerors were not allowed to confiscate property suggest about the Muslim view on spreading Islam? (*Possible answer: The Muslims were more concerned with protecting their religion than taking over property and creating a political empire.*)
2. What did the Umayyads have to gain from the death of Husayn? (*Possible answer: They could avoid any future threat that Husayn would want to lead the Muslims. They also clearly had to fear Husayn as a serious rival since he was Muhammad's grandson.*)
3. Why didn't some Arab Muslims consider non-Arab Muslims to be equal with them? (*Possible answer: Non-Arab Muslims were not from the same cultural background; they did not speak the same language; the Arab Muslims preferred collecting the non-Muslim tax from them*)

SOCIAL SCIENCES

Economics The third Pillar of Islam required that all Muslims pay a *zakat*, or charitable tax. Non-Muslims were required to pay a special tax called a *jizya*. Encourage students to research what the tax money was used for and how these taxes helped to keep the Muslim community running.

READING AND LANGUAGE ARTS

Reading Nonfiction Ask students to read the third paragraph of the chapter about the controversy surrounding the choice to make Uthman the next caliph. Have students pick out the main idea of the paragraph and list the details that support it.

THEN and NOW

Twice a year, many Muslims make the journey to Husayn's tomb in Karbala, Iraq. They travel barefoot to show their faithfulness on the days when Muslims traditionally mourn their dead.

LINKING DISCIPLINES

Math Every year, based on their lunar calendar, Muslims pay *zakat*, or charitable tax. This tax is to be paid at a rate of 2.5 percent of the total worth of a person's possessions and income. Have students calculate *zakat* for various values. Students might also want to investigate if other religions demand tithing or a tax of some kind, and how that amount compares monetarily with *zakat*.

LITERACY TIPS

In addition to using the suggestions in the Supporting Learning and Extending Learning sections, refer back frequently to pages 16–19 for strategies and advice from a literacy coach.

READING AND LANGUAGE ARTS CONTINUED

Using Language Point out that the word *tax* can be used as either a noun or a verb. Have students point out the various ways the word is used in the chapter. Then ask students to make a list of other words they know that can be used as a noun or a verb.

WRITING

Dialogue Discuss with students the controversy surrounding the choice of Uthman as the Islamic leader after Umar. Then have students form pairs and write a dialogue between someone who supported Uthman and someone who supported Ali as the next leader after Umar, giving specific examples about why the person they support should be the next leader. Students should pass a piece of paper back and forth, responding to each other in writing. Invite pairs to perform their dialogues.

SUPPORTING LEARNING

English Language Learners Have students work in pairs to read sections of the text and ask each other questions to review the material.

Struggling Readers Ask students to use the timeline graphic organizer (see reproducibles at the back of this guide) to show the order of leadership of the Muslims and the years these people led, as described in the chapter.

EXTENDING LEARNING

Enrichment The chapter discusses how some of the Christian Byzantines were easily converted to Islam because of the similarities between the two religions. Have students research the fundamental beliefs of the Christian and Muslim religions and create a Venn diagram showing the similarities and differences of the two religions.

Extension The chapter says that Muslims called Ali "imam" rather than "caliph." Have students find the meaning of "imam" and look for other names of leaders of the Muslim faith and their meanings.

NAME   **DATE**

MANAGING THE EMPIRE

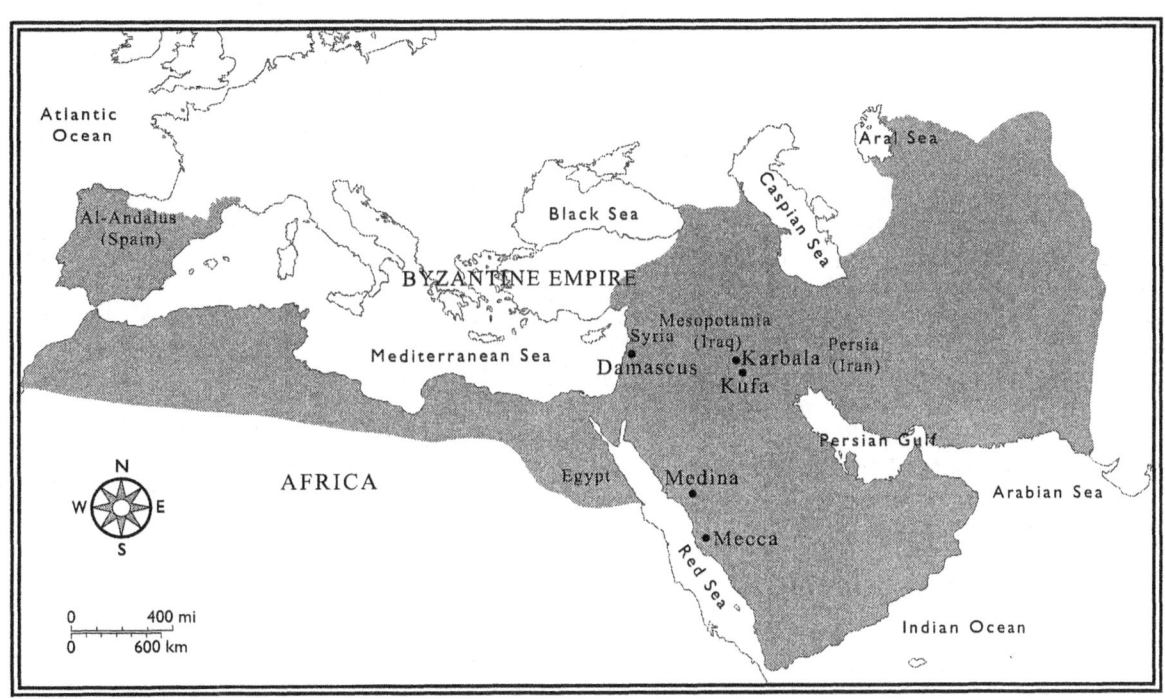

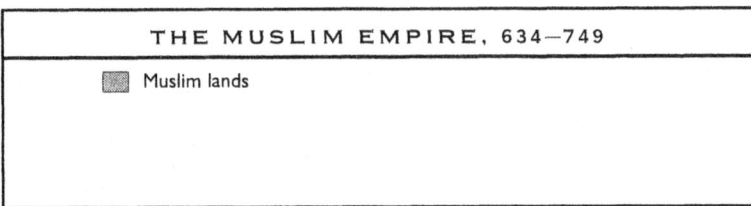

Directions

Study the map showing the Muslim Empire from 634–749. Use information from the chapter to add symbols to the map and key for the directions given below.

1. Add a symbol to the map and key to show the location of the battle between Muawiyah's and Ali's armies.

2. Add a symbol to the map and key to show the location of the new capital as chosen by Muawiyah.

3. Add a symbol to the map and key to show the location of Husayn's tomb.

PRIMARY SOURCES

Directions

Read the quote from al-Tabari below. Then answer the questions that follow.

> A man of the tribe of Madhhij killed [al-Husayn] and cut off his head. He took it to Ubaydallah [the governor of Iraq] and said:
>
> Fill my saddlebag with silver and gold,
> For I have killed the well-guarded king.
> I have killed the man of noblest parents,
> And when people trace descent his is best.
>
> [Ubaydallah] sent him to . . . Mu'awiyah [the Caliph] and with him he sent the head . . . [Mu'awiyah] began to poke the mouth with a cane . . .
>
> [Someone] cried out to him, "Take your cane away. By God! How often have I seen the apostle of God kiss that mouth!"

1. What does the man of the Madhhij tribe request?

2. Why does he make this request?

3. How does this man describe al-Husayn? What does he mean by this description?

4. Why does someone cry out and demand that Mu'awiyah remove the cane from al-Husayn's mouth?

5. Why is this description of the killing of Muhammad's grandson so historically important?

CHAPTER TEST 4

THE AFRICAN & MIDDLE EASTERN WORLD, 600–1500

A. MULTIPLE CHOICE

Circle the letter of the best answer to each question.

1. What was the *jizya*?
    a. the third pillar of Islam
    b. a charitable tax paid by Muslims
    c. the military camps where Muslims lived
    d. a special tax paid by non-Muslims

2. Which leader collected and published God's messages to Muhammad?
    a. Umar
    b. Uthman
    c. Muawiyah
    d. Ali

3. Ali was
    a. the Muslim leader after Muawiyah.
    b. killed by a Christian slave.
    c. the last elected caliph.
    d. a member of the Umayyad family.

4. Why did Muawiyah move the Muslim capital to Damascus?
    a. The tribes of Syria supported him.
    b. He feared for his life.
    c. Damascus was closer to Mecca.
    d. There were too many rebellions elsewhere in the Islamic Empire.

5. *Mawalis* were
    a. taxes paid by Muslims.
    b. Arab Muslims.
    c. Muslim converts.
    d. members of the Umayyad family.

B. SHORT ANSWER

Write a paragraph on the following subject.

6. Discuss some of the positive and negative reactions to the leadership of Uthman.

_____
_____
_____
_____
_____
_____
_____

C. ESSAY

Under Umayyad rule, a number of factions and divisions developed. Choose either the Shiites or the *mawalis* (non-Arab converts to Islam) and describe their relationship to the Umayyads in an essay. Conclude your essay with a description of how these two groups joined forces to challenge the Umayyads.

CHAPTER 5

THE HOUSE OF ISLAM: THE FIRST WORLDWIDE CIVILIZATION
(PAGES 55–67)

FOR HOMEWORK

STUDENT STUDY GUIDE
pages 27–30

CHAPTER SUMMARY

As the Abbasids began to take control as the leading group of Muslims, the Islamic capital was moved to Baghdad in Iraq. Baghdad grew rapidly and became an important center for trade. As trade expanded and leaders began to move farther from Baghdad, political power began to move to the hands of the sultans, while caliphs continued as spiritual leaders.

PERFORMANCE OBJECTIVES

- To explain how the Abbasids took control of the Muslim empire from the Umayyads
- To explain how Islam went from being an Arab religion to a multi-cultural religion
- To understand the importance of trade to the growth of the Muslim empire
- To explain how political control of the Muslim empire shifted to the hands of the sultans

BUILDING BACKGROUND

Ask students to think about the government buildings in their town or city. Have them discuss why the location of these buildings is important. Are they near the center of the city or town? Are they close to the water? Explain that they are going to read about how Baghdad and its palace developed as an important symbolic and economic center of the Muslim empire.

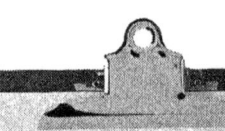

CAST OF CHARACTERS

Ibn Battuta (but-TOO-tuh) Berber from Tangier, Morocco, who left an account of his 75,000-mile journey throughout the Islamic world

Al-Mansur (al-man-SUHR) Abbasid caliph who supported Persian literature at his court and founded Baghdad

Fatima (FA-tuh-muh) daughter of Muhammad and wife of Ali

VOCABULARY

descendants those people who are related to or come from a group of people

geographic related to a certain region or area

radiating spreading out from a central point

provinces smaller territories of a larger area

lavish abundant or excessive, having too much

ornate highly decorated

As needed, have students consult the glossary to define the following words: *Abbasids, caliphs, clan, imam, Islam, jizya, Kharijites, mawalis, Muslims, Quran, Seljuk, Sharia, Shiite, Sunna, tribe, Umayyad.*

WORKING WITH PRIMARY SOURCES

Ibn Battuta lived during the first half of the 14th century. His accounts of his travels through Asia and Africa have been invaluable primary sources for information about the Islamic world during that time. For example, have students look at Ibn Battuta's description of the port of Aden on pages 59-60. Ask them to discuss what this quotation tells us about life in the ports of Arabia and what the people were like. The *Primary Sources & Reference Volume* also provides an account of another traveler in the region, Al-Masudi, who traveled in Persia, as well as in India, China, and East Africa around 915. Read "How to Catch an Elephant" to students and discuss any points of interest students might have.

GEOGRAPHY CONNECTION

Location Abu Jafar al-Mansur built a new Islamic capital in Baghdad in 622. Have students study the map and take note of the location of Baghdad. Ask them to share ideas about why this location would be beneficial to the growth of the Muslim empire.

READING COMPREHENSION QUESTIONS

1. What did the Abbasids do when they took over the Muslim empire to make Islam a way of life around the world? (*They stopped collecting the jizya from non-Arab Muslims* (mawali) *and allowed them to hold government office and positions in the army.*)
2. Why did al-Mansur make the city of Baghdad round? (*He thought it would be good for the king to be in the exact center.*)
3. As Baghdad grew, what were some things the caliphs did to make their government work? (*They installed a post office and spy network, hired translators, divided the empire into provinces and chose a governor for each, etc.*)
4. What was life like for the caliphs in their empire at this time? (*They lived a very luxurious life with many servants, wore luxury items of gold and silver decorated with jewels, and were clothed in fine fabrics.*)
5. Why did the caliphs come to rely on the Turkish slave armies? How did this dependence backfire on the caliphs? (*Muslims in provinces distant from the capital began to form new competing caliphates, which the caliphs wanted to stop. So the caliphs used professional, Turkish, slave armies to fight against these other groups. However, the Turks ended up taking political power away from the caliphs.*)

CRITICAL THINKING QUESTIONS

1. What benefit did al-Mansur gain from moving the Islamic capital to Baghdad? (*He was able to rule from a location that was a strong center for trade because of its location on the Tigris River and in the center of the Muslim empire. Putting it in a part of the empire that was ethnically less Arab also symbolized for many the new, multi-ethnic character of the Islam the new caliphal dynasty represented.*)
2. How did Kharijite and Shiite movements demonstrate that the Abbasid caliphate did not represent the interests of all Muslims? (*Possible answer: The Kharijite movement opposed the hereditary control of the caliphate by just one family, and the Shiites believed that only the direct descendents of Fatima [Muhammad's daughter] should lead the Muslim community.*)
3. How do you think the caliphs felt when the Turks took political power away from the caliphs? (*Possible answer: They were upset to lose power over the people and to not be able to control them politically. However, they were happy to still influence the religious lives of their followers.*)

SOCIAL SCIENCES

Sociology The chapter describes the role of a carpet maker's wife in Baghdad as one of modesty and responsibility to family. Have students discuss the role of these women in Baghdad in comparison with the role of women in their community today. Have students write comparison and contrast essays on the topic.

READING AND LANGUAGE ARTS

Reading Nonfiction Read aloud the second paragraph of the chapter to students before they begin reading the chapter. As you read, have students draw conclusions about the traits and values of the Abbasids. Later, have students compare their initial conclusions with further information they learn about the Abbasids.

THEN and NOW

The governing body of Iraq was once a caliphate and then a sultanate. Today, the government of Iraq is moving toward a democracy.

LINKING DISCIPLINES

Art/Architecture Have students read the description of al-Mansur's palace complex on page 56 and individually sketch images of the complex based on the written description. Then divide the class into small groups to compare their sketches. Discuss the similarities and differences between students' images. For homework, have students research examples of Muslim architecture from the Abbasid Empire. (Students can look in the library or on the Internet for examples.) Have them share their findings and lead a discussion about common architectural elements of the time period.

LITERACY TIPS

In addition to using the suggestions in the Supporting Learning and Extending Learning sections, refer back frequently to pages 16–19 for strategies and advice from a literacy coach.

READING AND LANGUAGE ARTS *CONTINUED*

Using Language Review the paragraph describing the palaces of the caliphs on page 60. Have students create a mental image of the description and explain which words in the paragraph helped them to create this image in their minds. Then have students draw their interpretations of the interior of a caliph's palace.

WRITING

Postcard Perspectives Have students review the many places Ibn Battuta visited during his travels. Divide students into small groups and explain to them that each group will be choosing a specific location from Ibn Battuta's travels from which to send a postcard home to his loved ones back in Morocco. (Of course postcards did not exist during this time, but this exercise aims to have students write from the perspective of Ibn Battuta—a worldwide explorer of Islamic lands.) After groups have determined their geographic locations in Ibn Battuta's travels, they can conduct further research on the lifestyles of the inhabitants of those places for homework (via the Internet or by visiting the library). Groups should then use class time to illustrate the front of the postcard with a scene that Ibn Battuta might have witnessed in their group's location. The back of the postcard should be a letter home from Ibn Battuta; the content of the letter could focus on what it was like to travel to that location and witness the scene depicted on the postcard. Students may also choose to date and stamp their cards (with stamps featuring a ruler of the time period). This project could culminate with oral presentations of the postcard projects.

SUPPORTING LEARNING

English Language Learners There are many examples of expressions or idioms used in the text such as "out-of-the-way places," "second-class citizens," "way of life," and "penny-pinching cheapskate." Have students work in pairs to find and explain these expressions.

Struggling Readers Students may benefit from the use of the timeline graphic organizer (see reproducibles at the back of this guide) to organize the information in the chapter. Ask students to skim the chapter, looking for dates. Then have them place these dates on a timeline and write a brief description of what happened during each year. For example, students might write "al-Mansur moves Muslim capital to Baghdad" for the year 662.

EXTENDING LEARNING

Enrichment Have students investigate the Seljuk Turks and their origins and history. Ask students to draw a map of the Abbasid Empire prior to the Seljuk Turks' rise in power. (Students can model their map after the map on Student Edition page 55.) Then have students shade in the areas of their maps where the Seljuks eventually gained control. Some useful websites include:
www.turkeytravelplanner.com/TravelDetails/History/Seljuks.html;
http://countrystudies.us/turkey/5.htm;
http://mb-soft.com/believe/txh/seljuk.htm.

Extension The chapter describes the industries that Ibn Battuta might have seen springing up in the Muslim empire as he traveled through Iraq, Persia, China, Egypt, and Syria. Ask students to work in pairs to research some of the other industries found in the Muslim empire during that time. Later, partners can orally present their findings to the class.

NAME _____ DATE _____

THE HOUSE OF ISLAM: THE FIRST WORLDWIDE CIVILIZATION

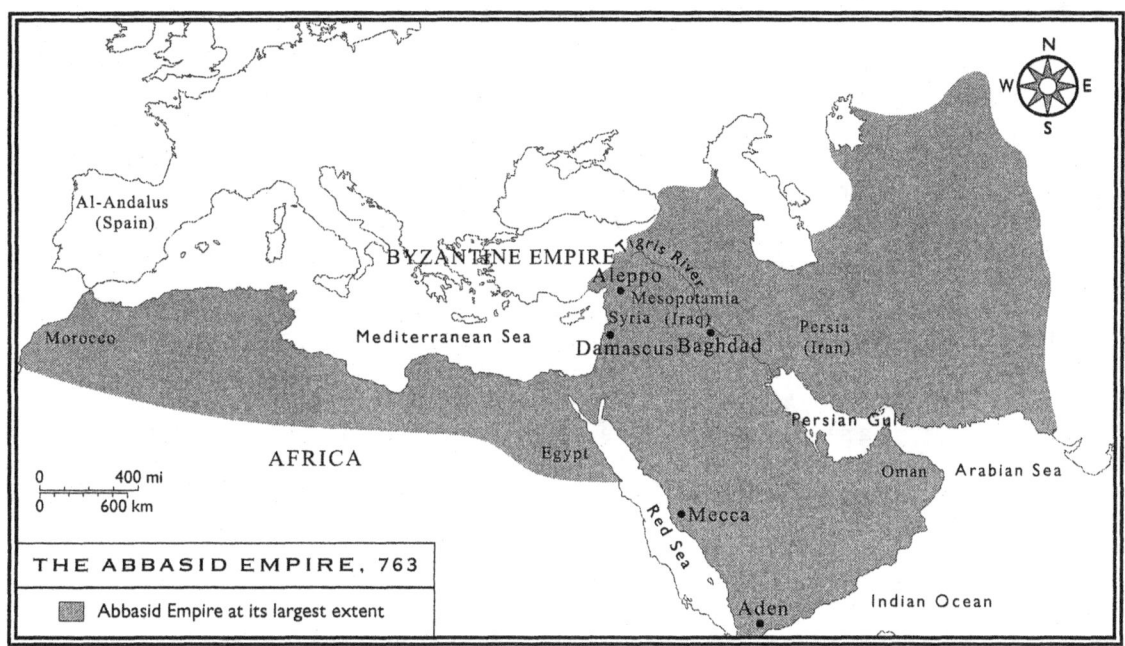

Directions

Study the map showing the Abbasid Empire in 763. Answer the questions and use information from the chapter to add symbols to the map and key for the directions given below.

1. Draw a star in the location of the new capital of Iraq as chosen by Abu Jafar al-Mansur.

_____
_____
_____

2. How might this location be beneficial to the empire?

_____
_____
_____

3. Draw a circle around the location of the seaport where large ships filled with luxury items were brought to the Arabian Peninsula from East Africa.

_____
_____
_____

4. Why is this a good location for a port?

_____
_____
_____

CHAPTER 5 BLM   AFRICAN & MIDDLE EASTERN WORLD, 600–1500   **53**

PRIMARY SOURCES

Directions

Read the two passages below. The first passage is from the Quran, regarding the treatment of slaves. In the second passage, Ibn Batutta tells of his observations of the treatment of a slave in Damascus.

> There is a clue which [God] presents to you from your own relationships. Would you . . . regard the slaves in your hands as participants with you [in your religion], as if you and they were equals respecting it? Do you hold them in the same sort of respect that you have for one another?
> —The Quran

> One day as I went along a lane in Damascus I saw a small slave who had dropped a Chinese porcelain dish, which was broken to bits. A number of people collected round him, and one of them said to him, "Gather up the pieces and take them to the custodian of the endowments for utensils." He did so, and the man went with him to the custodian, where the slave showed the broken pieces and received a sum sufficient to buy a similar dish. This is an excellent institution, for the master of the slave would undoubtedly have beaten him, or at least scolded him, for breaking the dish, and the slave would have been heartbroken and upset at the accident.
> — Ibn Battuta

IN YOUR OWN WORDS

1. Explain how the passage from the Quran is lived out in the observations made by Ibn Battuta.

2. What does the Quran suggest about slaves that might have been considered a radical idea at the time?

CHAPTER TEST 5

THE AFRICAN & MIDDLE EASTERN WORLD, 600–1500

NAME   **DATE**

A. MULTIPLE CHOICE

Circle the letter of the best answer to each question.

1. When the Abbasids became the new caliphs they did all of the following **except**
   a. stop collecting the *jizya*.
   b. cut off support payments to all Arab tribes except Muhammad's descendants.
   c. keep Islam contained in Baghdad.
   d. allow Muslims of other cultures to have privileged positions in the government and army.

2. Al-Mansur moved the capital to Baghdad because
   a. it was in the center of the Muslim empire.
   b. there was a large palace there.
   c. it would not cost too much money to build there.
   d. the city was round.

3. The best description of the way the caliphs in Baghdad lived is
   a. they lived modestly with only what they needed.
   b. they spent their days building palaces.
   c. they worked as merchants in the ports.
   d. they lived lives of luxury.

4. All of the following groups revolted against the Abbasids **except**
   a. abused slaves.   c. Shiites.
   b. Kharijites.   d. Persian *mawalis*.

5. What led to the end of the Abbbasid caliphate in Baghdad?
   a. Other Muslim clans revolted.
   b. The Turks took over political power.
   c. The Mongols destroyed the city.
   d. Oman opposed the caliphs.

B. SHORT ANSWER

Write one or two sentences to answer each question.

6. How did trade influence the Abbasid caliphate's power?

_____
_____
_____

7. What were the forces that led to revolts by the Kharijite and Shiite groups against the Abbasid caliphate?

_____
_____
_____

C. ESSAY

In an essay, discuss the developments in the Muslim empire during the Abbasid caliphate. Include details about how people under their rule lived and their relations with other groups.

CHAPTER 6

LIVING BY THE RULES: ULAMA AND PHILOSOPHERS
(PAGES 68–76)

FOR HOMEWORK

STUDENT STUDY GUIDE
pages 31–34

CHAPTER SUMMARY

The Abbasid caliphs encouraged people to discuss the teachings of Muhammad, and as a result groups of thinkers began to form, especially in the provinces of the Empire. These groups had their own interpretations of the Quran and practiced certain religious aspects of their daily life differently. A body of established Islamic customs and beliefs based on the living example of Mohammad was gradually compiled into a sacred book called the Sunna, which, taken together with the Quran, teaches Muslims how to live their faith.

PERFORMANCE OBJECTIVES

- To explain how Muhammad's teachings were followed during the Abbasid caliphate
- To describe the difference among the ideas of various scholars
- To understand how the Sufis helped to spread Islam

BUILDING BACKGROUND

Ask students to list the important books (e.g., Vedas, Hebrew Bible, New Testament) and the leaders of various religions (preacher, rabbi, priest, etc.). Discuss how these leaders help to interpret the important texts of their religions. To what degree do people turn to these leaders for guidance? How might the leaders use the information in the books to offer their guidance?

CAST OF CHARACTERS

Al-Ma'mun (al-mah-MOON) an especially well-educated caliph who supported the philosophical religious scholars known as the Mutazilites

Ahmad (AH-muhd) **ibn Hanbal** (HAHN-bahl) founder of one of the most important, and the most conservative, schools of Islamic law

Al-Ghazali (al-guh-ZA-lee) most respected religious scholar of his time; made Sufism, or Islamic mysticism, acceptable to orthodox scholars

VOCABULARY

piety state of being devoted to one's religion, being loyal

ijtihad intellectual struggle or reasoning used to deal with difficult situations

Students can also consult the glossary to define the following words:

Abbasids, caliphs, Five Pillars of Islam, hadiths, Islam, Muslims, Mutazilites, oral tradition, Quran, Sunna, Sufi, ulama.

WORKING WITH PRIMARY SOURCES

The poetry of Sufi writers tells much about the beauty and depth of their faith in God. Obtain copies of some Sufi poems by poets such as Rumi and read the poems aloud as students follow along. The Teacher Sourcebook includes a poem by the poet Omar Khayyám. Discuss the meanings of the poetry with students and have them share their ideas for how the poems represent the Sufis' beliefs. Poems by various Sufi poets can be found at *http://wahiduddin.net/sufi_poetry.htm*.

GEOGRAPHY CONNECTION

Interaction The chapter explains that through the Sufis' interaction with other groups, Islam spread beyond the borders of Arabia and Persia into Africa and South and Southeast Asia. Have students look at a map of this region and identify how far Islam spread through interaction with the Sufis.

READING COMPREHENSION QUESTIONS

1. Why did the Muslims feel lost after Muhammad's death? (*They thought Muhammad was a perfect Muslim but he did not leave instructions for many of the ways God wanted them to conduct their daily lives.*)
2. What are the hadith? (*They are the basis of the Sunna, which is the "way" of the prophet Muhammad. They are the accounts of how Muhammad lived that were passed down through oral tradition in the first two or three centuries after Muhammad's death. They are the basis of "Sunna" Islam, followed by the majority of Muslims.*)
3. Why were the ulama important? (*They settled issues of religion and daily living using a combination of the Quran, the hadith, and their own consensus views.*)
4. Why did the Mutazilites believe the Quran was not eternal? (*They believed that only God was eternal.*)
5. How did the Sufis focus on God? (*They chanted from the Quran, often while swaying forward and backward. They gave up their personal possessions, lived as beggars, and wore wool garments.*)

CRITICAL THINKING QUESTIONS

1. What do the hadiths of Muhammad that are quoted in the second paragraph tell you about how Muhammad expected people to treat each other? (*Possible answer: Muhammad expected people to treat each other with kindness and compassion and to greet each other in peace.*)
2. Why did ibn Hanbal's refusal to take al-Ma'mun's oath cause the religious authority of the Mutazilites to diminish? (*Possible answer: Hanbal was the most highly respected religious scholar of the age and had many loyal followers who would likely rebel against the caliph if he enforced the belief. Also, the Mutazilites' views were widely unpopular, and the refusal of such a respected scholar legitimized and served as a focus of popular opposition.*)
3. Why do you think the Sufis were so successful in helping the spread of Islam? (*Their religious practices included dance and music, which were popular religious elements of other cultures. This made the Islamic practices of the Sufis seem more familiar and comfortable to the new Muslims.*)

SOCIAL SCIENCES

Science, Technology, and Society Ibn Battuta described some of the extreme abilities of the Sufis when they were in a trance-like state of spirituality. Some were able to roll in and even eat fire. There are many cultures and societies around the world that use meditation and trance to help them focus on their spirituality. These include some Native American cultures, Buddhist and Hindu cultures, and some Haitian groups as well.

THEN and NOW

Unlike the Abbasid caliphate, the United States today separates church and state. This means that the laws of any particular religion do not influence the laws created by the government.

LINKING DISCIPLINES

Arts Have students reread the section on page 75 of the Student Edition that explains how the Sufis helped expand the Islamic world into Africa and South and Southeast Asia through their acceptance of dance and music as forms of worship. Then have them choose some aspect of this larger topic to research and present: for example, Sufi dance and its connections to Sufi spiritual beliefs; how Sufism spread in a particular country or region; or the evolution of Sufi music.

LITERACY TIPS

In addition to using the suggestions in the Supporting Learning and Extending Learning sections, refer back frequently to pages 16–19 for strategies and advice from a literacy coach.

READING AND LANGUAGE ARTS

Reading Nonfiction Have students use a paired oral summary strategy to review the chapter immediately after they have read it. First, pair students and have them decide who will be "speaker" first and who will be "listener." Next, give the speakers two minutes to tell the listeners everything they remember about the chapter (without looking back at the text). Listeners take notes, and interrupt only if something the speaker says is confusing or unclear. Have the pairs then switch roles so that the new speakers talk for another two minutes about anything they can add to the summary, while the listeners takes notes. Finally, have the pairs combine their notes and create short summaries of the chapter to read aloud to the class (consulting the text at this point if they need to). As pairs read their summaries, have the class identify aspects of the chapter that were noted in common.

Using Language The hadiths were stories about what Muhammad said or did that were passed down through oral tradition. Explain to students that oral tradition means that the stories are passed on by word of mouth from generation to generation and are not written down. Have students share stories or lessons that they have learned from grandparents or other family members that are passed on orally.

WRITING

Personal Narrative Point out that sometimes people try to convince us to do something we do not agree with. In the Chapter, al-Ma'mun wanted Ahmad ibn Hanbal to take an oath with which he did not agree, and so he refused. Ask students to write a short narrative about a time when someone tried to convince them to do something they did not agree with and have them tell how they responded.

SUPPORTING LEARNING

English Language Learners Have students use the main idea map graphic organizer (see reproducibles at the back of this guide) to organize the ideas from the chapter. Ask them to write *Living by the rules of Islam* and then, in the detail circles, write examples of how Muslims interpreted and used the rules of their religion to guide the way they lived.

Struggling Readers Have students make a two-column chart with the headings *ulama* and *Mutazilites*. Ask students to list the characteristics of each group under the appropriate heading.

EXTENDING LEARNING

Enrichment The chapter discusses the ideas of the religious scholars, the ulama, and how these scholars helped people interpret religious texts. Have students choose a religious scholar from history and write down a few ideas this person had.

Extension Assign students to work in pairs to choose a world religion and research how the beliefs, customs, rituals, and laws of that faith are passed down to and made understandable to children. (Because this information might vary by country or culture, students might choose to research how that faith is passed down in a particular community or part of the world.) For example, what special services or schools, coming-of-age rituals, holiday celebrations, or other customs are designed to teach children the faith? Have students create a chart or poster to display this information. Students might then compare similarities across the faiths represented.

CHAPTER 6

NAME   **DATE**

LIVING BY THE RULES: ULAMA AND PHILOSOPHERS

Directions

Use the Venn diagram below to compare and contrast the two essential books of Islamic belief, practice, and law, the Quran and the Sunna. (You may also want to also review earlier chapters that focus on the Quran.) Consider the origins and purposes of both books.

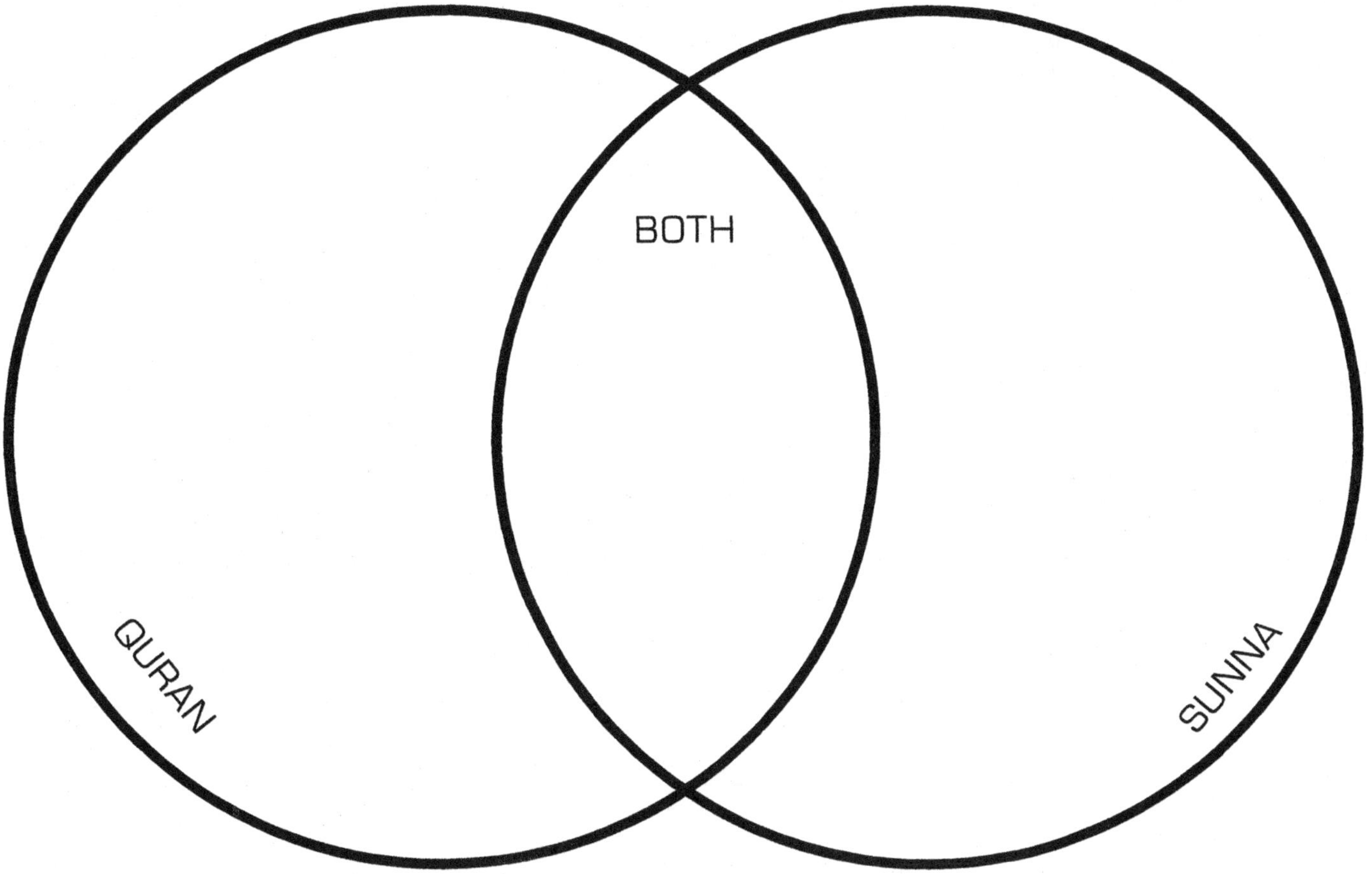

PRIMARY SOURCES

Directions

Jalal ad-Din al-Rumi is a well-known 13th-century Sufi poet. His poems are about the love and beauty of God. Read the poem below. Then answer the questions that follow.

> Come and be Love's [God's] willing slave,
> for Love's slavery will save you.
> Forsake the slavery of this world
> and take up Love's sweet service.
> The free, the world enslaves,
> but to slaves Love grants freedom.
> I crave release from this world
> like a bird from its egg;
> free me from this shell that clings.
> As from the grave, grant me new life.
> O Love, O quail in the free fields of spring,
> Wildly sing songs of joy.

1. In the poem, who is the "Love" to whom Rumi refers?

2. According to Rumi, why should someone choose to become Love's slave?

3. A simile is a comparison of two things using the words *like* or *as*. Rumi uses a simile to compare his desire for release from the world to something else. To what does Rumi compare this desire?

4. Write your own simile for desiring to be released from something that is confining you.

CHAPTER TEST 6

THE AFRICAN & MIDDLE EASTERN WORLD, 600–1500

NAME   **DATE**

A. MULTIPLE CHOICE

Circle the letter of the best answer to each question.

1. A hadith was
   a. an account of the things that Muhammad had said or done.
   b. a discussion and debate about the Quran.
   c. a decision about a person's guilt or innocence.
   d. a judge in Muslim courts.

2. While the Quran stresses moral principles and guidelines about piety and justice, the Sunna was established to
   a. give guidelines specifically about children.
   b. record Muslim legal cases.
   c. provide detailed teachings for daily living.
   d. record sacred writings only for ulama.

3. The thinkers called Mutazilites refused to
   a. swear the Quran was not eternal.
   b. disagree with religious scholars.
   c. follow the rules of Islam.
   d. recognize anyone as free from sin.

4. What did Ahmad ibn Hanbal refuse to do?
   a. follow the Five Pillars of Islam
   b. take an oath stating that the Quran was not eternal
   c. rebel against the caliph
   d. become an ulama

5. Ways that Sufis practiced their religion included all of the following **except**
   a. wearing woolen garments.
   b. working as legal scholars.
   c. living as beggars.
   d. spending time alone reading the Quran.

B. SHORT ANSWER

Write a paragraph to answer the following question.

Muhammad said, "You will not enter Paradise unless you are kind to each other, unless you warmly say salam [Peace] to each other whenever you meet." Write a paragraph explaining the meaning of these words and an example of how a Muslim might follow them.

C. ESSAY

The Quran and the Sunna are the primary sources of Islamic beliefs, practice, and law, and greatly influence Muslims' daily life. Write an essay that uses information from the chapter to tell how the Sunna originated and how it is different from the Quran.

CHAPTER 7

HOUSES OF WISDOM: ISLAMIC ARTS AND SCIENCES
(PAGES 77–90)

FOR HOMEWORK

STUDENT STUDY GUIDE
pages 35–38

CHAPTER SUMMARY

The Muslim world made great and important contributions to the fields of art and science. Many of the great Muslim thinkers influenced scientists and philosophers throughout history. Many Muslims traveled in search of knowledge. Through their search for knowledge, Muslims learned much and spread their own knowledge and culture.

PERFORMANCE OBJECTIVES

- To learn about the discoveries and observations of specific Muslim scholars and thinkers
- To understand the impact that Muslim thinkers had on the arts and sciences of the world
- To trace how the ideas of early Muslim thinkers were spread through Africa and Europe

BUILDING BACKGROUND

Invite students to name some of the famous inventors and scientists they have heard of. Ask them to share what they know about these people's lives and work. Have them also discuss how these people's inventions or thinking affected future inventions and life today. Explain that the chapter they will be reading is about some of the great Muslim scientists, philosophers, and artists who have had a great impact on ideas all over the world.

CAST OF CHARACTERS

Abu (uh-BOO) **Bakr** (BACK-er) **Muhammad** (moo-HAH-mud) **ar-Razi** (ar-RAH-zee) Persian physician

Al-Biruni (AL-bee-ROO-nee) Arab scholar of history, geography, medicine, chemistry, mathematics, and astronomy

Ibn Rushd (ROOSHT) Andalusian scholar most noted for his commentaries on the works of Aristotle

VOCABULARY

imposed put upon, made to do something

embarked began or set out on, as if on a journey

speculated meditated or thought about in a serious way

observant paying close attention

theory a belief or set of thoughts about a topic

scriptures a group of sacred writings to which people turn for guidance

bequeathed handed down

As needed, have students consult the glossary to define the following words: *Abbasids, Andalusian, Arabic, Bedouin, Berbers, caliphs, hadiths, House of Wisdom, Islam, Muslims, Quran, rihla, Sufi, shaykh, zejel.*

WORKING WITH PRIMARY SOURCES

The Muslim scholars and scientists discussed in this chapter recorded their thoughts and observations so that others could learn from them. In the *Primary Sources & Reference Volume*, there is an account of a Muslim geographer from Spain, Abd al-Aziz al-Bakari, who wrote a famous book about traveling in Ghana. Read the article "Tourist Guide to Ghana" to students. Discuss with students how al-Bakari's account might have been helpful to travelers in Ghana.

GEOGRAPHY CONNECTION

Region Ask students to look at the map on page 81 and point out the important Muslim cities included on the map. Have students name these cities according to the different regions in which they are located: Europe, Africa, and the Middle East. Then discuss why each of these locations was important in Muslim history.

READING COMPREHENSION QUESTIONS

1. What divine instruction did the Abbasid caliphs take seriously? (*Through Muhammad, God instructed Muslims to believe that searching for knowledge was a sacred duty.*)
2. What observation did ar-Razi make that made him associate hay fever with pollen? (*He noticed that people sneezed more in the springtime when the roses were blooming.*)
3. What observations about how society changes did Abu Zayd ibn Khaldun make? (*He observed that all civilizations go through a cycle of birth, greatness, decline, and disintegration.*)
4. To what extent did Ibn Battuta travel? (*He is considered one of the most highly traveled men of his time. He visited Mecca seven times and trekked the Islamic world from Spain to China and from southern Russia to East and West Africa.*)
5. How did Muslim literary figures influence later literary works by westerners? (*Edward Fitzgerald translated some of Omar Khayyám's poetry for a western audience; British novelist Daniel Defoe was influenced by Ibn Tufayl's work* Alive, Son of Awake.)

CRITICAL THINKING QUESTIONS

1. How did Ibn Tufayl and Ibn Rushd see the relationship between philosophy and religion differently? (*Although they both thought that philosophy and religion are related, Ibn Tufayl showed this idea through stories, or literary examples, and Ibn Rushd showed this idea through logical explanations.*)
2. What are the long lasting effects of the intellectual accomplishments of the Muslim scientists and philosophers discussed in the chapter? (*Possible answers include: al-Haitham's work on optics was translated into Latin and had an impact on Western scientists such as Kepler and Bacon; Razi's encyclopedia became a reference tool for European doctors; Ibn Khaldun's work influenced Karl Marx; Ibn Rushd's work inspired Thomas Aquinas, etc.*)

SOCIAL SCIENCES

Science, Technology, and Society Inform students that the Muslim physicist al-Haitham's research into the nature of light led him to experiment with the principle of camera obscura, where a tiny hole or lens in an otherwise darkened chamber will project an image of the view outside of the chamber onto a surface in the darkened room. Divide students into small groups and have them research the principle of camera obscura and how it has influenced artists in their techniques for homework. Then have them reconvene in class to create How It Works posters to explain how camera obscura works. Have each group orally present their posters and explain how the camera obscura may have aided famous artists (e.g., Da Vinci, Vermeer, Canaletto, etc.).

THEN and NOW

What was once called al-Andalus is now Spain. Today, the major religion practiced in Spain is Catholicism. Roman Catholics make up about 94 percent of the population. The other 6 percent includes Muslims, Jews, and Protestants.

LINKING DISCIPLINES

Art The caption on page 89 states: "The Quran forbade artists to represent human beings, because that was considered to be idol worship. So, for many centuries, art took the forms of abstract, geometric designs . . ." Have students research Islamic art during this time period and contrast it to later abstract and geometric works of art (e.g., works of art by Picasso or Miro). Students can make collages of sample works to illustrate their findings.

LITERACY TIPS

In addition to using the suggestions in the Supporting Learning and Extending Learning sections, refer back frequently to pages 16–19 for strategies and advice from a literacy coach.

READING AND LANGUAGE ARTS

Reading Nonfiction The chapter details the ideas and discoveries of some important Muslim scholars and scientists. Have students organize this information in a three-column chart. In the first column, have students list each person mentioned in the chapter. In the second column, have them list the important contributions of each person. For example, for ar-Razi, students might list accomplishments such as: wrote about human anatomy and diseases, associated hay fever with springtime, provided treatments, wrote an encyclopedia, and determined where to build a hospital. Students will fill in the third column in the Using Language activity.

Using Language Ask students to review the chapter, paying close attention to the descriptive words used to describe the people who are mentioned. Have students list these descriptive words in the third column of the chart they made in the Reading Nonfiction activity. Then discuss with students why these qualities would be important for the person to have in order to accomplish what he did. For example, for ar-Razi, students might list careful, observant, and practical. If the text does not provide descriptive words for a person, have students think of their own adjectives and descriptive words that might apply to that person.

WRITING

Interview Ask students to imagine they are a reporter who is assigned to interview one of the people discussed in the chapter. Have them choose a person from the chapter and write *who, what, when, where, why,* and *how* questions they would like to pose to the historic figure. Then have students write answers that their interviewee might have given in response to the questions they have written. Later, students can orally present their mock interviews in pairs.

SUPPORTING LEARNING

English Language Learners Ask students to make a list of the different sciences and fields of study mentioned in the chapter, such as philosophy, astronomy, anatomy, biology, architecture, art, literature, and geography. Then ask them to work in pairs to look these titles up to determine what is studied in each field. Encourage them to look for examples of these titles or names in their other readings. What do common suffixes such as *–omy* or *–ology* mean?

Struggling Readers To summarize the contributions of Muslim scientists and philosophers, have students make a two-column chart with the headings *Contributions in Science* and *Contributions in Thought* and list the people and the contributions they made in each of these areas.

EXTENDING LEARNING

Enrichment Since it is believed that the British novelist Daniel Defoe was inspired by Ibn Tufayl's work *Alive, Son of Awake,* have students use Ibn Tufayl's work to inspire them to write fictional short stories based on the same premise (a young child is reared on a deserted island by animals).

Extension The chapter mentions the influence of Arab and Berber cultures on the music of Spain. Have students listen to some music samples from each culture. Have students visit websites for information on flamenco and Iraqi music or to find free music samples to download www.iraqiart.com/songs/index.asp and www.flamenco-world.com/magazine/about/que_es_flamenco/indice11112004.htm.

CHAPTER 7

NAME   **DATE**

HOUSES OF WISDOM: ISLAMIC ARTS AND SCIENCES

Study the map showing the important cities for Islamic art and science between the 9th and 14th centuries. Then use information from the chapter to follow the directions below.

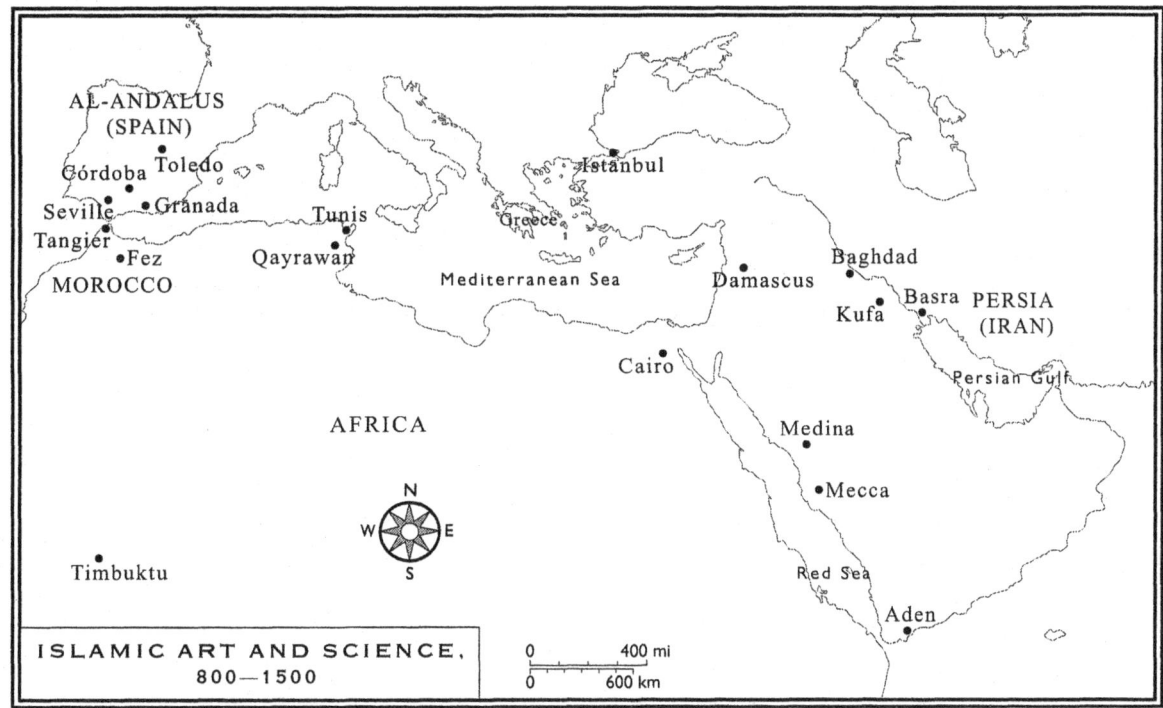

1. Draw a red triangle around the city where the House of Wisdom was located.

2. Draw a blue circle around the city where the hospital that ar-Razi helped set up was located.

3. Draw an orange star on the cities that were considered the main centers of Islamic thought.

4. Draw a purple square around the cities that were considered the primary centers of intellectual and cultural life.

5. Draw a green circle around the city where Ibn Battuta came from.

6. Draw a yellow triangle around the location of the Alhambra fortress.

HOUSES OF WISDOM: ISLAMIC ARTS AND SCIENCES

Directions

Read this excerpt of *Alive, Son of Awake*, written during the 12th century by Andalusian author Ibn Tufayl, and then answer the questions that follow.

> The doe felt sorry for the infant and nuzzled him tenderly. She gave him her udder and let him drink her own delicious milk. She became his constant nurse, caring for him, raising him and protecting him from harm. . . .
>
> When they went out to forage and came back to rest they were accompanied by a troop of deer that went along to graze and stayed the night near where they slept. Thus the child lived among the deer, imitating their calls so well that eventually his voice and theirs could hardly be distinguished. In the same way he imitated all the bird calls and animal cries he heard with amazing accuracy . . . The animals were used to him and he was used to them, so they were not afraid of each other.

1. How would you describe the doe's treatment toward the child when he was an infant?

2. How did the child show that he had adapted to the environment in which he was raised?

3. What reason does Ibn Tufayl give for the lack of fear that existed between the animals and the child?

NAME   **DATE**

A. MULTIPLE CHOICE

Circle the letter of the best answer to each question.

1. Al-Ma'mun built the House of Wisdom because
   a. he wanted to surround himself with scholars.
   b. he wanted to have a way for the hadith about knowledge to be fulfilled.
   c. he needed a larger house for Muslim scholars.
   d. he wanted to attract the best scholars to translate important texts into Arabic.

2. Al-Haitham's studies
   a. helped people find the best place for a hospital to be built.
   b. led to the translation of important texts into Arabic.
   c. led to an understanding of hay fever.
   d. influenced the work of Johannes Kepler and Francis Bacon.

3. All of the following are true of ar-Razi **except**
   a. he went blind because of a disease.
   b. he discovered the smallpox and measles were two different diseases.
   c. he compiled an encyclopedia of medical knowledge.
   d. he wrote about human anatomy and many diseases.

4. What is a *zejel*?
   a. a verse of poetry on the theme of love
   b. an entry from Ibn Battuta's travel journal
   c. a Spanish song
   d. a fountain decorated with lions' heads

5. Arab and Berber cultures gave Spain all of the following **except**
   a. the guitar and castanets.   c. Christianity.
   b. the Arabic language.   d. flamenco dancing.

B. SHORT ANSWER

Write one or two sentences to answer each question.

5. How did Al-Haitham's scientific experiments influence later works of research?

_____
_____
_____

6. What is a *rihla* and how did this concept guide Ibn Battuta's life?

_____
_____
_____

C. ESSAY

In an essay, explain how Muslim writers contributed to the field of literature. Your examples should explain how particular contributions influenced later works of literature by non-Muslim writers.

CHAPTER 8

NOW IT'S ISTANBUL, NOT CONSTANTINOPLE: THE OTTOMAN EMPIRE (PAGES 91–102)

FOR HOMEWORK
STUDENT STUDY GUIDE
pages 39–42

CHAPTER SUMMARY

After centuries of trying to conquer Constantinople, the Muslims finally invaded Manzikert in 1071, which led to further advancement into the Byzantine Empire. Through the next centuries, the Ottomans continued the take-over of Anatolia (Turkey) and the Balkan Peninsula, through to Vienna, Austria.

PERFORMANCE OBJECTIVES

- To trace the sequence of events through the rise and fall of the Ottoman Empire
- To identify some important historical figures of the Ottoman Empire
- To understand new methods of warfare used by the Ottomans to conquer more territory in southeastern Europe and the Near East.

BUILDING BACKGROUND

Initiate a class discussion about times in history when groups of people tried to expand the borders of their nation. As examples, remind students of ancient Rome and even the United States. Ask them to share their ideas about how and why people choose to expand their nation as well as the impact this expansion might have on the people or land that is being taken over.

VOCABULARY

sovereignty a control over government

siege a blockade of a city to force it to surrender

vizier a high executive officer

As needed, have students consult the glossary to define the following words: *Bedouin, Byzantine, caliphs, devshirme, harem, Islam, Janissaries, Ka'ba, Muslims, Seljuk, shaykh, Shiite, Sunnis, Topkapi, tribe, ulama*.

CAST OF CHARACTERS

Osman (os-MAHN) founder of the Ottoman Empire

Mehmed II (MEH-meht) Ottoman sultan who brought Byzantine Empire to an end when he conquered Constantinople

WORKING WITH PRIMARY SOURCES

Long before the Ottoman armies took Constantinople for their empire in 1453, the city was a wealthy and active center for trade. The *Primary Sources & Reference Volume* provides an account of a traveler, Benjamin of Tudela, in Constantinople in 1174. Read "Bright Lights, Big City" to students and discuss any points of interest students might have.

GEOGRAPHY CONNECTION

Place Ask students to review the description of the Suleymaniyya Mosque in the chapter. Point out that this structure still stands as one of the most magnificent buildings in Turkey. Students might enjoy finding more information about the mosque. Some helpful websites include:
www.greatbuildings.com/buildings/Suleyman_Mosque.html,
www.metu.edu.tr/home/wwwissch/ozgurey/istanbul/suleymaniye.htm, and
www.enjoyturkey.com/info/sights/suleymaniye.htm

READING COMPREHENSION QUESTIONS

1. What did the Seljuk Turks do in 1071? (*They defeated the Byzantines at the Battle of Manzikert in northern Syria and started the Muslim advance into Anatolia.*)
2. What did Osman ask of his son Orhan? (*He asked that Orhan keep fighting to take more lands and spread Islam.*)
3. What problem did John Comnenus have? (*He had asked Orhan to help him win the Byzantine throne, but Orhan and the Ottomans did not leave and used their position to invade southeastern Europe.*)
4. What was the *devshirme*? (*The devshirme was the "harvest" of boys. Starting under Sultan Murad II, the Ottoman Turks took the strongest and smartest Christian boys from their families, forced them to convert to Islam, and educated them to perform military and administrative services for the sultan.*)
5. How did the Ottomans finally defeat Constantinople? (*They had developed cannons made of brass or bronze that were powerful enough to blow apart the walls of the city.*)

CRITICAL THINKING QUESTIONS

1. What type of leader was Osman? (*He was a charismatic leader who was able to inspire his people to defeat the enemies of Islam. But he was not very well-organized, ruling without a formal administration and relying instead on sufi ("dervish") brotherhoods to organize and govern his followers.*)
2. Explain what caused Suleyman the Magnificent to withdraw from public life. (*He led a magnificent empire with many wives and sons. One wife, Roxelana, was jealous of the heir to the empire, Mustapha. She led Suleyman to believe that Mustapha was plotting against him and so Suleyman killed Mustapha. Roxelana also had Suleyman's best friend and advisor killed. The loss of these two important people in Suleyman's life caused him great sadness and to withdraw from public life.*)

SOCIAL SCIENCES

Civics The text states that Orhan did just what his father, Osman, asked of him on his death bed. Have students list the actions Orhan took to make sure he would be successful. For example, Orhan created an organized state and chose a capital for the sultanate.

READING AND LANGUAGE ARTS

Reading Nonfiction Give students examples of cause-and-effect statements. For example: Because the Seljuk Turks were a strong military force, they were able to defeat the Byzantines. Have partners review the chapter. One partner should write down the *cause* part of a sentence; the other partner should complete the sentence with the *effect*.

THEN and NOW

The new technology used to make cannons in the 15th century led to the defeat of Constantinople by the Ottomans. Today, cannons are called autocannons. They can fire rapidly and can be fired from moving vehicles such as aircraft and tanks.

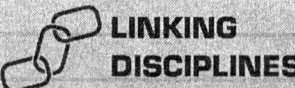

LINKING DISCIPLINES

Science If it were not for the advancement in cannon technology, the Ottomans may not have been able to advance beyond Constantinople. Have students think of inventions that have been improved through technology. For example, the computer replaced the typewriter. Have students work in groups to make a list of as many inventions as they can think of that have been made better through technology.

LITERACY TIPS

In addition to using the suggestions in the Supporting Learning and Extending Learning sections, refer back frequently to pages 16–19 for strategies and advice from a literacy coach.

READING AND LANGUAGE ARTS CONTINUED

Using Language The chapter is full of words that relate to war and conflict is some way. Have students review the chapter and make a list of these words in their history journals. They can then compare their lists with a partner and work together to use the words in sentences. Some examples include *defeat*, *defend*, and *conquest*.

WRITING

Ask students to reread the description of the Suleymaniyya Mosque in the chapter. Then ask students to think of a beautiful or interesting building they have been to. Have them write a brief description of that building and analyze how its architectural features affect visitors. Ask volunteers to read their descriptions to a small group of students.

SUPPORTING LEARNING

English Language Learners Help students list the words in the text that have to do with being a leader and leadership, such as sultan, governor, and authority. Have students then work in pairs to brainstorm more words that have to do with leaders and leadership (perhaps concentrating on those specific to our own culture and government). Finally, have them look up the words they do not know, and create a word web that shows the relationships between all the words they have listed.

Struggling Readers Have students use the timeline graphic organizer (see reproducibles at the back of this guide) to show the order of important events discussed in the chapter.

EXTENDING LEARNING

Enrichment Students can use maps to learn more about how the Ottomans gained control of the Balkan Peninsula. A variety of maps showing the history of the Balkan Peninsula can be found at the website *http://balcanica.org/history/maps.html*.

Extension Have small groups of students work together to write a skit about one of the events in the chapter. For example, students may choose to act out Osman's final conversation with Orhan, the events between Roxelana and Suleyman, or the people's reaction to the *devshirme*. Then have students perform their skits for each other.

NAME   **DATE**

NOW IT'S ISTANBUL, NOT CONSTANTINOPLE: THE OTTOMAN EMPIRE

Directions

Use the information from the map below and in the chapter to answer the questions that follow.

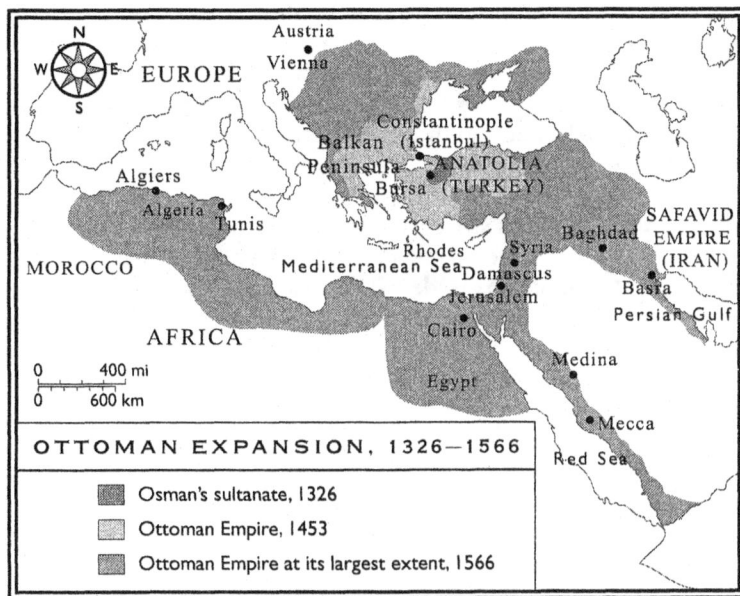

1. What was the location of the Battle of Manzikert?

   _____

   Draw an "X" at this location.

2. Which city did Orhan name as the capital of his sultanate?

   _____

   Draw a circle around this city.

3. Which prized city did Mehmed take for the Ottoman Empire in 1453?

   _____

   Draw a triangle around this city.

4. Which city, which Suleyman was unable to conquer, was the capital of the Austrian Empire?

   _____

   Draw a square around this city.

PRIMARY SOURCES

Directions

The first passage below is a description of the Seljuk Turks as written by Abu Ali al-Tanukhi. The second passage is a description of the Ottoman sultan and his army as written by Kritovoulos. Read the passages. Then answer the questions that follow.

I. [T]he Turk will hit from his saddle an animal, a bird, a target, a man, a crouching animal, a marker post or a bird of prey stooping on its quarry. His horse may be exhausted from being galloped and reined in, wheeled to the right and left, and mounted and dismounted: but he himself goes on shooting, loosing ten arrows before [another] has let fly one.

II. . . . pressing on up to the palisade. After a long and bitter struggle, [the Ottomans] hurled back the [Byzantine defenders] from there and climbed by force up the palisade. They dashed some of their foe down into the ditch between the great wall and palisade, which was deep and hard to get out of, and they killed them there. The rest they drove back to the gate.

1. Based on the first passage, what type of warriors were the Seljuk Turks?

2. What are three adjectives that you would use to describe the Ottoman army?

3. Based on the passages, in what ways are the armies similar?

4. Based on the passage, how are the armies different?

CHAPTER TEST 8

THE AFRICAN & MIDDLE EASTERN WORLD, 600–1500

A. MULTIPLE CHOICE

Circle the letter of the best answer to each question.

1. The Seljuk Turks accomplished all of the following **except**
    a. they defeated the Byzantines at the Battle of Manzikert.
    b. they established the Rum sultanate.
    c. they appointed Osman as governor of a province of Anatolia.
    d. they took Baghdad from the Hulegu Mongols.

2. During Osman's sultanate,
    a. there was a well-organized government.
    b. the sultanate had grown to include most of northwestern Anatolia.
    c. the *ghazi* state grew very little.
    d. Osman remained loyal to the Rum sultanate.

3. All of the following are true of Orhan **except**
    a. he was the son of Osman.
    b. he launched a successful invasion into southeastern Europe.
    c. he was a faithful friend to John Comnenus.
    d. he created an organized sultanate with the capital at Bursa.

4. *Devshirme* boys were not
    a. taken from their families.
    b. forced to convert to Islam.
    c. eventually the elite forces of the Ottoman armies.
    d. allowed to leave the palace during their training.

5. Mehmed managed to take Constantinople because
    a. he had new cannons that were made of bronze and brass.
    b. Constantinople did not have strong walls around its borders.
    c. the armies in Constantinople did not try to fight back.
    d. Mehmed's army was from Constantinople.

B. SHORT ANSWER

Write one or two sentences to answer each question.

6. What happened as a result of Orhan's giving each commander of the mounted warriors his own estate?

7. What was the effect of the Ottoman armies' being equipped with guns?

C. ESSAY

Describe the reign of "Suleyman the Magnificent" under whom the Ottoman Empire reached its greatest size. Include details from the chapter including his military accomplishments, the ways he supported the growth of religion, and the problems in his family life.

CHAPTER 9

WHERE GOLD GROWS AS CARROTS DO: GHANA AND THE AFRICAN GRASSLANDS (PAGES 103–113)

FOR HOMEWORK

STUDENT STUDY GUIDE pages 43–46

CHAPTER SUMMARY

The people of West Africa, Berbers and people of the grasslands, traded items they acquired in their homelands. This trade made towns wealthy and led to the development of kingdoms such as Ghana, where gold was in great supply. The wealth in Ghana drew many people to the area, including Muslim Berbers who brought salt to trade, as well as the religion of Islam.

PERFORMANCE OBJECTIVES

- To identify the medieval kingdoms of West Africa
- To explain how trade led to the rise of kingdoms such as Ghana
- To understand the spread of Islam to West Africa

BUILDING BACKGROUND

Ask students if they have ever traded anything with friends. Invite them to discuss some of the items they may trade, such as baseball cards, music CDs, or items from their lunches. Have them explain how they determine what makes a fair trade. Explain that this chapter discusses how trade in West Africa helped kingdoms to develop.

CAST OF CHARACTERS

Tunka (TUNGA-ka) **Manin** (MA-nin) king of Ghana

Abdallah (ub-duh-LAH) **ibn Yasin** (yah-SEEN) Moroccan Islamic scholar who led, until his death, a holy war called the Almoravid jihad

VOCABULARY

chiefdom an area or group ruled by a chief

dehydration a physical condition defined by lack of water

Ghana Soninke term for "king"

grassland a semiarid region with few trees, more suitable for raising livestock than cultivating crops

millet a type of grain

As needed, have students consult the glossary to define the following words: *Allah, Almoravids, Arabic, Berbers, imam, Islam, jihad, Kharijites, Muslims, Quran, ribat, Sahel, Sanhaja, Shiite, Sunnis, Soninke, tribe.*

WORKING WITH PRIMARY SOURCES

Have students look at the African creation story in paragraph three of the chapter. Read these sentences aloud and then ask students to share their thoughts on how this story is similar to and different from other creation stories they have heard.

GEOGRAPHY CONNECTION

Interaction Help students recognize that the interaction between the Berbers and the people of the grasslands led to the development of cities and kingdoms. Point out that the availability of salt and gold in the West African region made this a wealthy area, which also contributed to the cultural growth and change there.

READING COMPREHENSION QUESTIONS

1. What was the region that the Berbers lived in like? (*The region included the Sahara Desert and received little rain. To the south of the desert, in the Sahel, there was some grassland area filled with wild game for hunting.*)

2. What was one of the risks to caravans traveling in the desert? (*They could get lost far from water and could die.*)

3. Why did farmers southwest of Ghana dig for gold? (*They sometimes needed the gold to trade for salt, cloth, and other items they could not make themselves.*)

4. How were the kings of Ghana greeted? (*They were announced with trumpets and drums, and people approached them on their bellies while sprinkling dust on their heads.*)

5. Why did Ibn Yasin resort to force against the Berbers? (*The Berbers had rejected Ibn Yasin's form of Islam, Sunni Islam, and chose to stay with their own forms of Islam, Shiite and Kharijite Islam.*)

CRITICAL THINKING QUESTIONS

1. How do you think the Ghana might have felt about the special treatment he received? (*Possible answer: He might have enjoyed the special treatment because everyone was always taking care of him, but he also may have felt that it was a lot of responsibility; he also may have gotten bored of not being able to be like everyone else.*)

2. Why do you think that the conversion of the kings of Ghana to Islam contributed to Ghana's decline? (*Possible answer: The conversion to Islam that took place undermined the kings' authority as divine kings. During the Islamic holy wars, the kings' strength was tested. Though they were not actually invaded by the Almoravids, their conflict with the Almoravids probably weakened the kings' authority and encouraged rival chiefs to the south to rebel.*)

SOCIAL SCIENCES

Economics Review the paragraphs of the chapter that discuss the economic improvements, including the growth of kingdoms that took place in West Africa as a result of trade. Have students speculate about how trade could lead to such improvements and growth. For example, interaction with a variety of people could mean that people will learn new ways of doing things. As a related project, have students research how trade or industry has influenced their own community and local economy.

READING AND LANGUAGE ARTS

Reading Nonfiction Have students draw conclusions about the life of the Berbers and the people of the grasslands from the primary source materials within the chapter. They can organize their information into a two-column chart with a column dedicated to each group and its characteristics. For example, students should include in the column about the Berbers that they traveled from place to place, driving their camels to water. And in the column for the people of the grasslands, they should include that they lived settled lives in villages where they worked as farmers and herded livestock such as goats.

THEN and NOW

According to information gathered in 1985, the religious make-up of Ghana is 62 percent Christian, 15 percent Muslim, 21 percent traditional religions and 1 percent nonbelievers.

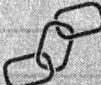

LINKING DISCIPLINES

Health If the Berbers got lost in the desert, they could perish from heat exhaustion or dehydration. Have students research the causes and symptoms of heat exhaustion as well as some of the ways of treating the condition. After they have completed their research, have students create informational pamphlets on dehydration that could be distributed in a medical clinic.

LITERACY TIPS

In addition to using the suggestions in the Supporting Learning and Extending Learning sections, refer back frequently to pages 16–19 for strategies and advice from a literacy coach.

READING AND LANGUAGE ARTS CONTINUED

Using Language The chapter uses many adverbs to explain how an action is done. Have students find examples of adverbs and tell how these words modify the verb. For example, in "gradually changes" the adverb "gradually" answers the question, "How did it change?" as, "It changed in a slow way over time." Point out that sometimes the adverb appears before the verb and sometimes it appears after the verb. Some adverbs and verbs may even be separated by other words.

WRITING

Explanation Read the paragraph about the items the caravans carried with them across the desert on page 105. Then, write a paragraph from the point of view of someone traveling on the caravan explaining why each item was important. Students can speculate about the origin of each item and its possible destination.

SUPPORTING LEARNING

English Language Learners Have students make a list of about five words from the chapter that they do not know. Then have them work in pairs to help each other figure out the meaning of the words from the context in which they were used or to look up the words in the dictionary.

Struggling Readers Have students work in pairs to review the chapter, pointing out and discussing the main idea of each paragraph as they review.

EXTENDING LEARNING

Enrichment Divide the class into small groups and have each group research a different topic related to Ghana. Topics could include but are not limited to: history, politics, religion, geography, and culture. You can find helpful websites on page 169 of the Student Edition. Students can collect their information and make oral presentations to the class about their topics. Some groups may like to make a chart, map, or poster as a visual aid for their presentations.

Extension The Ghana was greeted with special treatment such as trumpets and drums and people approaching on their bellies. Have students discuss the different rituals involved in the arrival of important heads of state or royalty in different countries. They can research in newspapers and magazines, if necessary, or share what they have seen on the news. Ask them to tell how this treatment is the same or different from the way the Ghana was treated.

NAME _____ DATE _____

WHERE GOLD GROWS AS CARROTS DO: GHANA AND THE AFRICAN GRASSLANDS

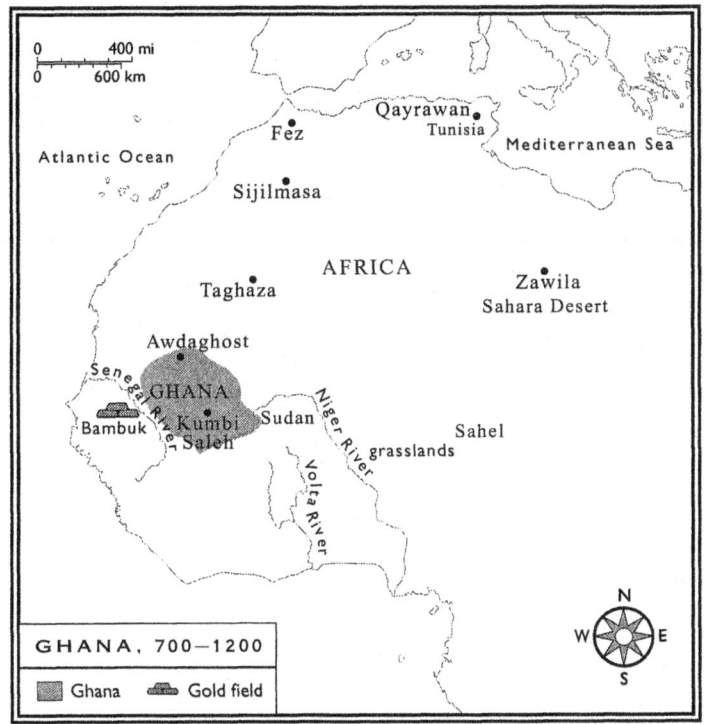

Directions

Use the information from the map below and in the chapter to answer the questions that follow.

1. In what region did the Berbers live?

   _____

   Write *Berbers* on the map in this area.

2. In what region did the people of the grasslands live?

   _____

   Write *people of the grasslands* on the map in this area.

3. Where did the Soninke people live?

   _____

   Write *Soninke* on the map in this area.

4. What city did Abdallah ibn Yasin come from?

   _____

   Draw a circle around this city.

5. How do the physical features of this geographic region influence the lives of its inhabitants?

   _____
   _____
   _____

CHAPTER 9 BLM   AFRICAN & MIDDLE EASTERN WORLD, 600–1500   **77**

PRIMARY SOURCES

Directions

Read the passage below. Then answer the questions that follow.

> Between Awdaghost [West Africa] and North Africa there is more than one tribe of isolated Berbers who have never seen a settlement and know nothing other than the remote desert. . . . They are steadfast and brave, good camel drivers, light-footed in running and tough. They know well the conditions and forms of the land and how to find their way over it, and how to be guided to water-points by description and discussion. . . . They have a sense of direction which no one comes near to except those who are close to them and lead the same life.

1. Circle any adjectives in the passage that are used to describe the Berbers.

2. Underline three of the skills that the Berbers have that are mentioned in the passage.

3. How do these skills help the Berbers live in the desert?

4. Why might the Berbers have such a good sense of direction?

CHAPTER TEST 9

THE AFRICAN & MIDDLE EASTERN WORLD, 600–1500

NAME   **DATE**

A. MULTIPLE CHOICE

Circle the letter of the best answer to each question.

1. What was life like for the people of the grasslands?
   a. They traveled constantly.
   b. They lived lives of hunting and farming.
   c. They raised camels.
   d. They traded items they brought from other areas of West Africa.

2. Traveling in a caravan was dangerous for all these reasons **except**
   a. the heat of the desert was very intense.
   b. travelers had to depend on water holes.
   c. it was possible to get lost in the desert.
   d. the journey took place at night.

3. How did the kingdom of Ghana get its name?
   a. It was the name of the divine kings who ruled.
   b. It was an important oasis for the Berber people.
   c. It was the name of a farming method of the people of the grasslands.
   d. It was the name of the king's mother.

4. The Ghana inherited his job from his
   a. father.
   b. mother's brother.
   c. mother.
   d. brother.

5. Why did Abdallah ibn Yasin go to the Sanhaja Berbers?
   a. He wanted to travel with them.
   b. He wanted to learn their religion.
   c. He wanted them to be obedient to strict Sunni Islamic principles.
   d. He wanted to attend the ribat.

B. SHORT ANSWER

Write one or two sentences to answer each question.

6. Why was Ghana in an ideal location for taking advantage of the gold trade?

7. How did trade bring change to medieval West Africa?

C. ESSAY

In an essay, describe the developments that led to Sunni Islam becoming the accepted form of Islam throughout North and West Africa after the 11th century.

CHAPTER 10

SADDLEBAGS STUFFED WITH GOLD: THE EMPIRES OF MALI AND SONGHAY (PAGES 114–128)

FOR HOMEWORK

STUDENT STUDY GUIDE
pages 47–50

CAST OF CHARACTERS

Sundiata (suhn-dee-AH-tah) fabled founder of the Kingdom of Mali

Mansa (MAHN-suh) **Musa** (MOO-suh) Mali's emperor known for his pilgrimage in which he distributed gold as gifts all along the route to Mecca

Mansa (MAHN-suh) **Sulayman** (soo-lay-MAHN) king of Mali who supported Islamic teaching at Timbuktu

Askia (as-KEE-yuh) **Muhammad** (moo-HAH-mud) **Turé** (too-RAY) Songhay emperor and founder of Askia dynasty

CHAPTER SUMMARY

After the fall of Ghana's empire, the Soninke kingdom was in power until 1235, when the area was named Mali. The Muslim leaders, or mansas, of Mali ruled a people who followed traditional beliefs. These mansas tried to convert the people to Islam but were not entirely successful. Songhay was another powerful empire. But over time, the rulers, called Askias, quarreled over leadership and were later defeated by a Moroccan army and weakened both the Mali and Songhay empires.

PERFORMANCE OBJECTIVES

▶ To understand the growth and decline of the Mali and Songhay empires
▶ To explain the leadership in the Mali and Songhay empires
▶ To describe the importance of gold to the rise of the Mali and Songhay empires

BUILDING BACKGROUND

Initiate a class discussion about other places in history where the discovery of gold led to the expansion of a nation and the immigration of a people, for example the Gold Rush in the United States. Ask them to share their ideas about why people would be so interested in settling where gold can be found and what benefit gold would have to the people who found it.

VOCABULARY

alliance a bond or connection between countries or groups

dignitaries people of honor or rank

prominent well-known

prosperity a condition of wealth or success

As needed, have students consult the glossary to define the following words: *Arabic, Berbers, Caliphs, clan, Five Pillars of Islam, ghazis, griots, Islam, caliphs, Mandinka, Mansa, Muslims, oasis, oral tradition, Quran, rainforest, Sosso, Soninke, Tuareg, ulama.*

WORKING WITH PRIMARY SOURCES

The Student Edition provides an introduction from a griot, or West African storyteller, about the brave leader Sundiata. Explain that the words of this passage were intended to be heard, as the tradition of telling stories is an oral tradtion. Read "Power Lies in Deeds" to students and have them share their thoughts on the devices this storyteller uses to get the listener involved in the story. For example, the griot begins his speech by saying, "But listen to what your ancestors did, so that you will know what you have to do."

80 | CHAPTER 10

GEOGRAPHY CONNECTION

Region Have students compare a map of present-day West Africa with the map of the Mali and Songhay Empires in their books. Have them discuss the countries that exist in this place today.

READING COMPREHENSION QUESTIONS

1. How was Sundiata able to carve out a large empire for himself? (*He created an alliance of chiefdoms that fought against the Sosso people and won the kingdom.*)
2. Why did the Mande people, who followed traditional religion, allow the Muslim mansas to rule over them? (*They believed the mansa were the "owners of the soil" and had a special connection with their nature gods and ancestral spirits. They wanted to keep their spirits and gods happy to assure themselves of good harvests and prosperity.*)
3. What traditional practice did Mansa Sulayman continue to follow even though it went against Islamic practice? (*He continued to have a Queen Mother at court who occupied an official position there, and she and the Mansa's wives continued to exercise power.*)
4. Why was Gao an important city to possess? (*Gao was an impressive city and the main trading link to the central and eastern Sahara.*)
5. Why did Muhammad Turé think that Islam was important to the trade of his people? (*He believed that Islamic law provided a framework for business and the Arabic language to improve communication with business partners from far away.*)

CRITICAL THINKING QUESTIONS

1. Why would Mansa Musa's giving gold away reduce the commercial value of gold? (*If too many people had gold, it would not be a precious or important thing to have anymore and so it would become less valuable.*)
2. How did the presence of the Moroccan army in Songhay impact trade? (*Trade suffered because there was increased warfare, which made it difficult for merchants to do business.*)

SOCIAL SCIENCES

Civics The Muslim leaders kept a balance between leading an Islamic kingdom and allowing the practice of traditional religions. Have students discuss the kinds of problems these leaders might have faced in trying to bridge the two.

READING AND LANGUAGE ARTS

Reading Nonfiction Have students preview the chapter by looking at the title, pictures, graphic aids, and sidebars. Have them discuss any points of interest and what they think the chapter will be about. They can write any questions they may have in the first column of a two-column chart and answer these questions as they read the chapter.

Using Language In the third paragraph, Timbuktu is described as having become the "central trans-Saharan caravan port." Explain that the prefix *trans-* means across. As a class, discuss the meaning of the word "trans-Saharan." Then, make a list of other words beginning with the prefix *trans-* and discuss each word's meaning.

THEN and NOW

Today, many of the manuscripts of Islamic law, theology, and history of early Timbuktu reside at the University of Sankore. Many of these manuscripts have been hand copied and the Ahmed Baba Center, opened in 1974, is home to 14,000 volumes.

 LINKING DISCIPLINES

Math/Statistics When Mansa Musa gave away too much gold, he decreased its value. Have students visit the website *www.gold.org/value/stats/statistics/daily short2000.html* to compare the value of gold in various currencies from around the world. Discuss what this means for the comparative value of each currency. For example, at a particular time, how many US dollars equal the same number of euros or yen based on the value of gold in that currency?

LITERATURE CONNECTION

Several versions of the Sundiata story are available, including Roland Bertol's *Sundiata: The Epic of the Lion King* (New York: Crowell, 1970), a retelling of the African epic in which an ugly, crippled child grew up to become the liberator and founder of the great empire of old Mali; and David Wisniewski's *Sundiata: Lion King of Old Mali* (New York: Clarion Books, 1992), the story of the man who overcame physical handicaps, social disgrace, and strong opposition to rule Mali in the thirteenth century. Other literary works about Sundiata and the empires of Mali and Songhay appear in the Further Reading section of the Student Edition.

LITERACY TIPS

In addition to using the suggestions in the Supporting Learning and Extending Learning sections, refer back frequently to pages 16–19 for strategies and advice from a literacy coach.

WRITING

News Article Have students work in small groups to use new articles from magazines and newspapers as models for writing a news article about one of the events in the article. For example, students may chose to write about the journey of Mansa Musa or the fight for control of Gao. Students may need to do further research on the Internet. Have them be sure to include the "who, what, where, when, why, and how" of the news, and write a headline to sum it up.

SUPPORTING LEARNING

English Language Learners The chapter is full of words that stand for a how a group of people can be joined together, such as *kingdom, chiefdoms, alliance, empire,* and *clan*. Have students work in pairs to find these words and any others make a list of them. Then, have them add to their lists by brainstorming words we use today in our own country for groups that are joined together. What similarities and differences can they find between the two lists?

Struggling Readers Have students use the sequence of events chart (see reproducibles at the back of this guide) to order the rulers mentioned in the chapter. Then have students write one important thing about each ruler in the corresponding boxes.

EXTENDING LEARNING

Enrichment The chapter discusses the Mande practice of passing things down through the mother's line and the official position of the Queen Mother at court. Have students choose a prominent woman in politics from the present or past and research her life, her leadership, and the various challenges she faced.

Extension Have students choose one of the rulers mentioned in the chapter and work in groups to do further research on that person using encyclopedias or the Internet (see sources on Student Edition page 169). Then have students share with the rest of the class what they have learned.

NAME   **DATE**

THE EMPIRES OF MALI AND SONGHAY

Directions

Use the information from the map below and in the chapter to answer the questions that follow.

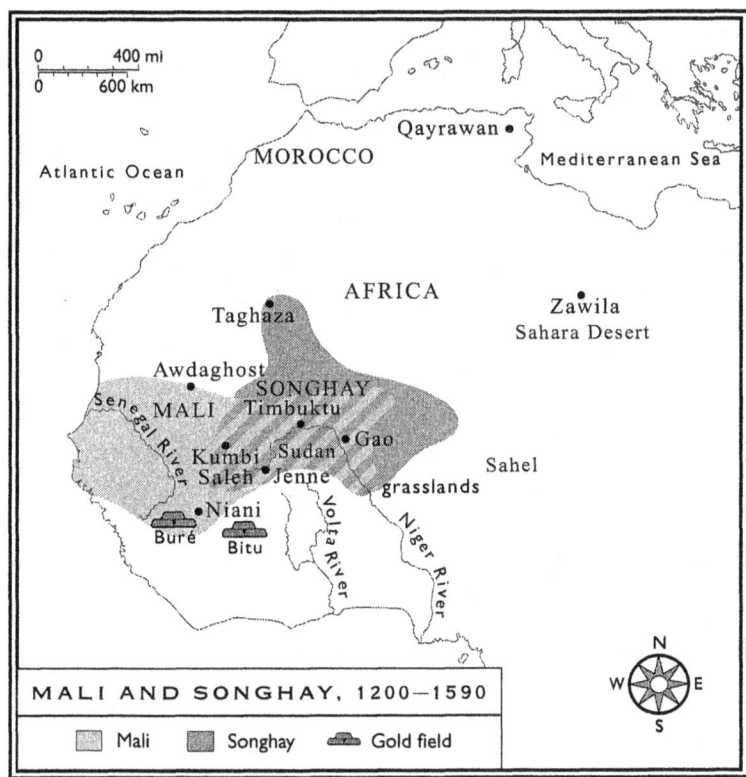

1. Which city was the capital of Sundiata's empire?

   Draw a star at the name of that city on the map.

2. In which two regions was gold found after the mines in Bambuk ran out?

   Draw a star at the name of that city on the map.

3. What was the location of Sankore Mosque University?

   Draw a box around the name of this city.

PRIMARY SOURCES

Directions

Read Ibn Battuta's description to Mansa Sulayman as he comes to meet his officials. Then answer the questions that follow.

> The sultan sits on certain days in the palace yard to give audience. There is a platform with three steps under a tree.... It is covered with silk and has pillows placed on it. The [screen] is raised, there is a shelter made of silk with a golden bird like a sparrowhawk above it.... The sultan walks slowly and pauses often and sometimes he stops completely. When he comes to the [screen] he stops and looks at the people. Then he mounts the steps with dignity in the manner of a preacher getting into the pulpit. When he sits down they beat the drums, blow the bugles and the horns, and three of the slaves go out in haste and call the deputy and the [commanders of the army]. They enter and sit down.... [The court translator] stands at the door while the rest of the people are in the street under the tree.

1. How has the palace yard been prepared for the sultan?

2. What three words can you think of that describe the sultan?

3. What do you imagine will be the people's reaction to Mansa Sulayman when he begins to speak? What in the passage gives you clues?

NAME   **DATE**

A. MULTIPLE CHOICE

Circle the letter of the best answer to each question.

1. All of the following describe the mansas **except**
   a. they were Mandinka kings.
   b. they continued some traditional Sudanese practices.
   c. they did not marry.
   d. the combined both kingly and religious powers.

2. Gold trading was responsible for all of the following **except**
   a. it brought Arab Muslims to Africa.
   b. it according to the farmers, pleased the gods and spirits.
   c. it enriched the city of Jenne.
   d. it brought Islam to Western Sudan.

3. All of the following are reasons for the fall of the Mali empire **except**
   a. the Mossi people attacked from the south.
   b. the leaders converted to Islam.
   c. the Tuareg people attacked from the northeast.
   d. there was a rivalry among several branches of the royal clan.

4. How did Muhammad Turé come to power?
   a. He was appointed by the ulama.
   b. He drove Sonni Ali's son from the throne.
   c. He was next in line for the throne.
   d. He founded the empire he ruled.

5. All of the following are reasons for the fall of Songhay **except**
   a. the Askias quarreled over succession.
   b. a Moroccan army attacked with guns.
   c. it became a center for trading slaves.
   d. there was so much war in the region that merchants could no longer do business.

B. SHORT ANSWER

Choose two of the following historical figures from the chapter and write a brief description of why each was important.

Sundiata   Mansa Musa   Mansa Sulayman   Sonni Ali   Muhammad Turé

_____
_____
_____
_____
_____

C. ESSAY

In the Empire of Mali, Mandinka kings (mansas) like Mansa Musa and Mansa Sulayman both encouraged their people to follow Islam and continued traditional Sudanese spiritual and cultural practices. On a separate piece of paper, write an essay in which you describe how and why they supported both these practices.

CHAPTER 11 — ONIS AND OBAS: THE FOREST KINGS OF WEST AFRICA
(PAGES 129–137)

FOR HOMEWORK
STUDENT STUDY GUIDE
pages 51–54

CHAPTER SUMMARY

The forest kingdoms of West Africa depended upon oral traditions that dictated religious practices and divine rulers. A divine king called the Oni ruled the Yoruba of the trading center of Ifé. Traders with forest products passed through Ifé, but most trade was local and depended on farming peoples who lived in the surrounding countryside. A divine king, the Alafin, ruled the Yoruba city-state of Oyo (1400–late-1700s). Benin's king, also considered divine, was called the Oba. An Oba named Ewuare was particularly powerful and wise. Obas made records of their reigns in bronze and brass—the renowned Benin bronzes. These bronzes provided insight into the nature of Benin kingship and culture.

PERFORMANCE OBJECTIVES

- To compare and contrast Yoruba and Bini rulers and customs
- To analyze trade patterns in West African forest towns
- To understand the importance of oral tradition in the West African forest kingdoms
- To summarize the contributions of rulers Ewuare and Oguola
- To evaluate the historic and aesthetic value of Benin bronzes

BUILDING BACKGROUND

Show students several photographs of Benin bronzes. After students react freely to the artwork, mention that Benin bronzes epitomize African art in the minds of many Westerners. Encourage students to find out how these sculptures originated and what they represent as they read the chapter.

VOCABULARY

lagoons shallow bodies of water separated from the sea

casting something shaped in a mold

As needed, have students consult the glossary to define the following words: *Alafin, Bini, clan, Islam, Oba, Oni, Oyo, oral tradition, Yoruba.*

WORKING WITH PRIMARY SOURCES

Students can examine photographs of bronze and brass sculptures from Benin on *www.zyama.com/benin/pics.htm*. To learn more about the discovery of Benin bronzes by Europeans and the subsequent history of the works, students can visit the Web site *www.arm.arc.co.UK/britishBenin.html*. Have students choose one Benin bronze to depict with a sketch in their notebooks.

CAST OF CHARACTERS

Ewuare (ewe-WAH-ray) the Great general and statesman who increased the power of the kingdom of Benin

GEOGRAPHY CONNECTION

Location Have students turn to the Forest Kingdoms map in Chapter 11 (page 130) or distribute the blackline master that has the map. Begin by having a volunteer identify the area shown on the Forest Kingdoms map on a larger map of Africa. Then ask students to compare the kingdoms discussed in this chapter—Ifé, Oyo, and Benin—with the other regions shown on the map, such as Timbuktu, Jenne, and Gao. Ask: How do the terrains differ? How would you compare these two regions' access to water?

READING COMPREHENSION QUESTIONS

1. What was the source of the power of rulers such as Onis, Obas, and Alafins? (*Their people believed that these rulers were divine.*)
2. What were two reasons that Ifé was a good place for trade? (*It was located between the forest and grasslands.*)
3. In what way were the forest kingdoms like the city-states of ancient Greece? (*Both were organized around their capital cities.*)
4. Why was Ewuare considered a great Oba? (*He expanded his kingdom, developed Benin City, and increased the power of the monarchy by taking away some inherited power of the nobility.*)
5. Who is credited with bringing the art of bronze and brass casting to Benin, and how did he do it? (*A Bini king, Oguola, had the Oni of Ifé send a brass-smith to Benin to create artworks and teach others the craft.*)

CRITICAL THINKING QUESTIONS

1. In what way did farming contribute to Yoruba civilization? (*The farms were productive enough to support great cities and large ruling and religious classes.*)
2. How do we know that the people of Benin were not Yoruba? (*They spoke a different language.*)
3. What function did the bronze and brass likenesses of Bini kings serve? (*The statues depicted their divinity and power.*)

SOCIAL SCIENCES

Economy Using the forest kingdom of Ifé as an example, let students discuss the importance of trade. If necessary, ask questions such as the following: How does trade permit civilizations to grow and to prosper? How does location determine the importance of trade to a community? In what ways does an extremely remote location and lack of trade limit a civilization?

READING AND LANGUAGE ARTS

Reading Nonfiction Help students identify the points of view of the authors and speakers quoted in this chapter. Make sure students understand how different the view from inside a society is, such as the description of Ewuare from the Bini oral tradition, from the view of an outsider, as in Richard Eden's description of a Bini king.

Using Language Have students list the adjectives used to describe the Bini Oba Ewuare and the verbs that show what actions he took. Have them use a main idea map like the one in the back of this guide. They should write *Ewuare* at the center and the adjectives and verbs in the other, smaller circles. Encourage them to add circles as necessary. Then have volunteers explain how these words contribute to their understanding of Ewuare's character.

THEN and NOW

The Benin bronzes were originally made for the people of Benin to celebrate the power and glory of their Obas. Now many of these famous bronzes are displayed in the British Museum and other museums in the West. Nigeria (the modern-day country which includes what was the kingdom of Benin) has repeatedly called for their return, but so far the British Museum has kept the bronzes. Which side do you support in this disagreement and why?

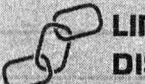

LINKING DISCIPLINES

Economics The Yoruba and many other Africans used cowry shells and metal bars as currency. Challenge students to find out what other items have been used as currency in various parts of the world. Then have students discuss the advantages and disadvantages of using such items as currency and why most of the world's population came to use paper currency and coins.

LITERACY TIPS

In addition to using the suggestions in the Supporting Learning and Extending Learning sections, refer back frequently to pages 16–19 for strategies and advice from a literacy coach.

WRITING

Expository Paragraph Have students research one of the trade goods that passed through Ifé, such as ivory or kola nuts. Then ask them to write an expository paragraph about the item they researched. Have students explain in detail what the item looked like and what it was used for, how it was gathered and transported, and why people valued it.

SUPPORTING LEARNING

English Language Learners Show students pictures of as many of the objects mentioned in the chapter as you can, including elephant tusks, kola nuts, yams, cowries, and so on. As you display each item, pronounce its name as you write it on the board. Encourage students to pronounce each name along with you. Have students refer to the list for help as they read the chapter.

Struggling Readers Have students make a two-column chart to list the names of important people and places as they read the chapter. The first column should contain the names of the important people and places, and the second column should contain details or further explanation regarding each item. After they finish reading, they can use their list to help them review the information they learned. If they are unable to identify a person or place on their list, they should locate the passage in the text that mentions that person or place.

EXTENDING LEARNING

Enrichment The Forest Kingdoms gave rise to a rich artistic tradition in Western Africa. Have interested students prepare an oral report for the class to tell more about the sculptures pictured in the book (and other pieces they find out about in their research). They should talk about artistic style as well as how the pieces were used in rituals and ceremonies.

Extension The Benin people had a long history of storytelling, but very little was written down from this oral tradition. Some compelling myths and stories survive, thanks to the efforts of anthropologists and historians. Have students investigate the range of Benin myths and royal accounts and share several notable examples with the class.

NAME _____ DATE _____

THE FOREST KINGDOMS, 1000–1500

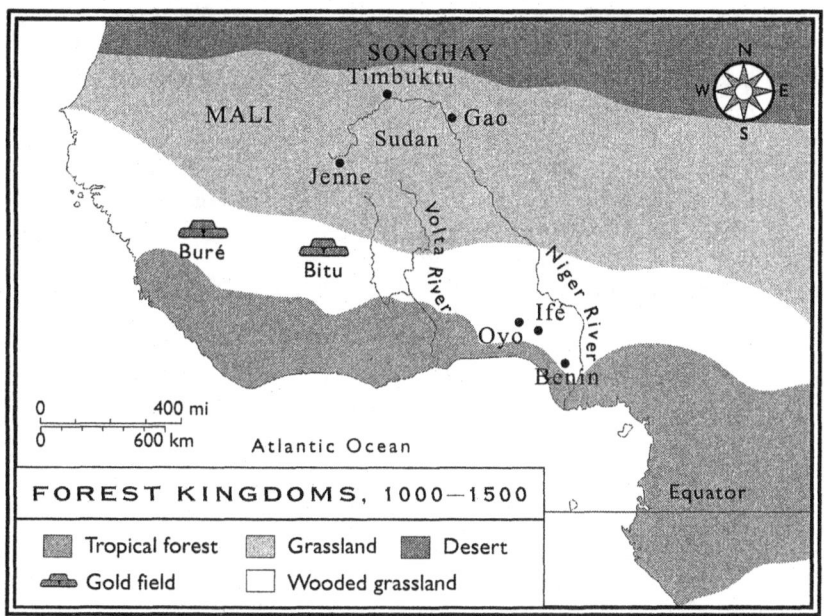

Directions

Study the map. Then use it along with information from the chapter to complete the items on this page.

1. Draw lines that show the routes trade items from Buré and Bitu took to end up in Jenne. Then figure out how great a distance the items traveled from each of these places.

   _____
   _____
   _____

2. Using the map, explain why Ifé was such a good spot for traders.

   _____
   _____
   _____

3. Compare a map of modern-day Africa with this regional map. Identify where each medieval town and city noted on the Forest Kingdoms map would be located today in Africa.

   _____
   _____
   _____

CHAPTER 11 BLM   AFRICAN & MIDDLE EASTERN WORLD, 600–1500

PRIMARY SOURCES

Directions

Read the quotations. The first is a description of Ifé that comes from a publication titled *Church Missionary Intelligencer*, which was published in 1854. The second is from the words of a Bini man, Chief Jacob Egharevba. Answer the questions using complete sentences.

> From thence flows, as from a fountain, all the water on the face of the earth, salt as well as fresh. From thence the sun and the moon arise, where they are buried in the ground, and all the people of this country, and even white men, have come from this town.

> Ewuare was a great magician, physician, traveler and warrior.

1. How would you judge the importance of Ifé to the Yoruba, and what function did it play in Yoruba religious beliefs?

2. The first quotation appeared in an English-language publication, *Church Missionary Intelligencer*. How might the intended audience have reacted to this origin tale?

3. Judging from the second quotation, how did Ewuare differ from many kings you have read about?

4. What hints can you gather about Bini culture from the description of Ewuare?

CHAPTER TEST 11

THE AFRICAN & MIDDLE EASTERN WORLD, 600–1500

NAME _____ DATE _____

A. MULTIPLE CHOICE

Circle the letter of the best answer to each question.

1. Which of the following was a word for king?
   a. Ewuare
   b. Odudwa
   c. Oguola
   d. Alafin

2. What was a manila?
   a. a vegetable
   b. an iron bar
   c. a kind of chief
   d. a cowry shell

3. Which factor did not contribute to Ifé's success as a trading center?
   a. being between the forest and grasslands
   b. being a city of well-educated people
   c. being on the route to Jenne
   d. being on the water

4. How would you describe the Alafin's power?
   a. slight
   b. nonexistent
   c. unlimited
   d. great

5. Which was an improvement Ewuare made to Benin City?
   a. plumbing
   b. new walls
   c. civic buildings
   d. statues of himself

B. SHORT ANSWER

Write one or two sentences to answer each question.

6. How did oral tradition play an important role in the forest kingdoms of West Africa?

_____
_____
_____

7. How do the Benin bronzes tell us a lot about the nature of Benin kingship?

_____
_____
_____

C. ESSAY

In an essay, compare and contrast Obas Ewuare and Oguola. Include details about how these rulers had similar duties but distinct characteristics.

CHAPTER 12

THERE'S TREASURE IN THOSE HILLS!: GREAT ZIMBABWE AND THE SHONA OF SOUTHERN AFRICA (PAGES 138–147)

FOR HOMEWORK
STUDENT STUDY GUIDE
pages 55–58

CAST OF CHARACTERS

Mutota (moo-TOW-tah) last-known king of Great Zimbabwe, who conquered the northern Shona people and established the Kingdom of Mwenemutapa

Mutope (moo-TOW-pay) king of Mwenemutapa around 1450–80; under his rule, Mwenemutapa grew to be the most powerful state on the Shona plateau

CHAPTER SUMMARY

Great Zimbabwe began as a farming area inhabited by Bantu people and grew wealthy through the raising and trading of cattle. Traders from the coast traveled to this area bringing goods. The area was abandoned, possibly because people moved to the Shona plateau where there were new sources of gold. It was trade in gold that led the Kingdom of Mwenemutapa to grow wealthy. However, the seizure of control of the costal trade by the Portuguese led to the decline of the kingdom.

PERFORMANCE OBJECTIVES

▶ To explain the development of Great Zimbabwe
▶ To understand the development of the Shona people and the Mwenemutapa kingdom
▶ To explain the importance of gold in the development of the Shona civilization
▶ To discuss the effects of trade in the Mwenemutapa kingdom

BUILDING BACKGROUND

Have students share what they know about farming and raising cattle in the United States. Ask questions such as: How are farms run? What crops are grown in what areas? Why are these crops grown in these places? Where is cattle raised? Why are these places good for raising cattle? Explain that students will be reading about a group of people, the Bantu, who were farmers and raised cattle.

VOCABULARY

plateau large land area with a level surface that is raised above an area of land on at least one side

enclosures structures meant to contain something

terraces a series of raised level platforms built to increase land cultivation, conserve moisture, or minimize erosion

As needed, have students consult the glossary to define the following words: *Bantu, clan, kraals, oral tradition, savannah.*

WORKING WITH PRIMARY SOURCES

Ask students to read the quotation of the Portuguese traveler who observed the gold mining of the Shona people on Student Edition pages 144-145. Then have students research how gold is mined today. Have them work in pairs to make a chart comparing the similarities and differences between the Shona system described and that of today. One helpful website is www.goldinstitute.org/mining/howchart.html.

GEOGRAPHY CONNECTION

Location Have students look at the map on page 142. Ask: What are the geographic characteristics of Mwenemutapa and Shonaland? (*They are located between two rivers and on the east coast of Africa.*) What benefit could these civilizations have because of this location? (*Possible answer: Goods can be transported more easily by rivers and oceans than overland.*)

READING COMPREHENSION QUESTIONS

1. How did the Bantu begin to acquire wealth? (*After living as a farming culture, the Bantu began hoarding cows, which they used for milk and meat as well as money in trading for other items.*)
2. How might the Bantu started to have chiefs? (*Conflicts between cattle breeders over land created the need for a third party to help settle the disputes. The chiefs filled this role.*)
3. What did the archeological finds from the site of Mapungubwe point to? (*Trade was a major source of wealth and power for the rulers there.*)
4. According to Shona oral traditions, what did the shortage of salt cause? (*Mutota, the last king of Great Zimbabwe left the city and went on to conquer Dande.*)
5. What did Matope do and what state was established as a result? (*He extended the northern capital and opened trade with the coast, then extended power over the northern Shona people and established the new state of Karanga.*)

CRITICAL THINKING QUESTIONS

1. How do we know that Great Zimbabwe and Mapungubwe were built by the same people? (*The stone-cutting technologies and construction techniques of the two places are similar.*)
2. Explain the causes of the decline of the kingdom of Mwenemutapa. (*The Portuguese seized control of the coastal trade and continued through the Zambezi Valley, claiming all the wealth for themselves and imposing taxes on the trade. Portuguese missionaries mistreated people because of their native religions. Kings no longer had wealth or power, and the kingdom fell.*)

SOCIAL SCIENCES

Science, Technology, and Society Zimbabwe means "stone buildings" in the Shona language. The structures and walls built in Great Zimbabwe were made from rectangular cut stones stacked in such a way that they have remained standing for hundreds of years. Have students research photos of these walls and discuss how they think these walls have stood the tests of weather ad time. Some helpful websites are *www.playahata.com/pages/bhfigures/bhfigures14.html* and *www.history.und.ac.za/ebe1mhm/zimbabwe.htm*.

READING AND LANGUAGE ARTS

Reading Nonfiction Remind students that when people read they make connections between what they read and their own experiences. Have students each find a passage in the text that reminded them of something they have heard or experienced. Then ask students to work in small groups to read the passage they chose and explain the connection they made with it.

Using Language Help students recognize that the chapter contains many geography words (for example, *coast*, *plateau*, *drought*, and *interior*). Have students work in pairs to find and define as many geography words as they can find in a given amount of time. Then have pairs share their list and definitions with the class.

THEN and NOW

Today the Shona people number 9 million and live in the countries of Zimbabwe and Mozambique. They are mostly farmers and raise some livestock. They also earn money by selling their arts and crafts.

LINKING DISCIPLINES

Art Even today, the Shona people are known for their beautifully carved head rests like the one pictured on page 146 of the student book. Have students research some images of these headrests and other arts, such as baskets and sculptures, of the Shona people. Have them work in pairs to collect some images of Shona arts as well as explanations of the uses and purposes of these items and share what they find with their classmates.

LITERACY TIPS

In addition to using the suggestions in the Supporting Learning and Extending Learning sections, refer back frequently to pages 16–19 for strategies and advice from a literacy coach.

WRITING

News Article Ask students to imagine that another set of *zimbabwe* walls have been discovered by archaeologists. Have them write a news article for a science and social studies magazine about the big discovery. They can use the research they have done in the other activities to help them fill out their articles with information.

SUPPORTING LEARNING

English Language Learners Have students read the section "City Made of Stone: Great Zimbabwe" beginning on page 141. Before they read, ask them to make a list of words that have to do with structures and building. After reading, ask students to work in pairs to find words that have to do with structures and building and organize the words on a two-column chart with the labels *Types of buildings* and *How buildings are made*. For example, in the first column, students might include words such as *buildings, structures, terraces,* and *walls*. In the second column, they might include words such as *stone-cutting techniques, construction,* and *built*. Encourage students to discuss these words by connecting them to the main ideas of the chapter.

Struggling Readers Ask students to use the sequence of events chart (see reproducibles at the back of this guide) to organize the information in the chapter. Ask students to include detailed information about each event they include on the chart.

EXTENDING LEARNING

Enrichment Students may enjoy working in groups to find out more about what archeologists have found out about life in Great Zimbabwe. Some helpful websites include:

www.globalheritagefund.org/where/nomination_zimbabwe.html,
www.archaeology.org/9807/abstracts/africa.html and
http://library.thinkquest.org/J001645/gzimb.shtml

Extension Ask students to find out more about the role of the Portuguese in southeastern Africa in the 15th and 16th century as well as why they came to that region in the first place. Students can organize the information they find into research presentations and present their findings to the class. Some helpful websites include:

www.bbc.co.uk/worldservice/africa/features/storyofafrica/10chapter3.shtml and
www.factmonster.com/ce6/world/A0859810.html.

NAME _____ DATE _____

SHONA CIVILIZATION, 1000–1500

Directions

Use the information from the map below and in the chapter to answer the questions that follow.

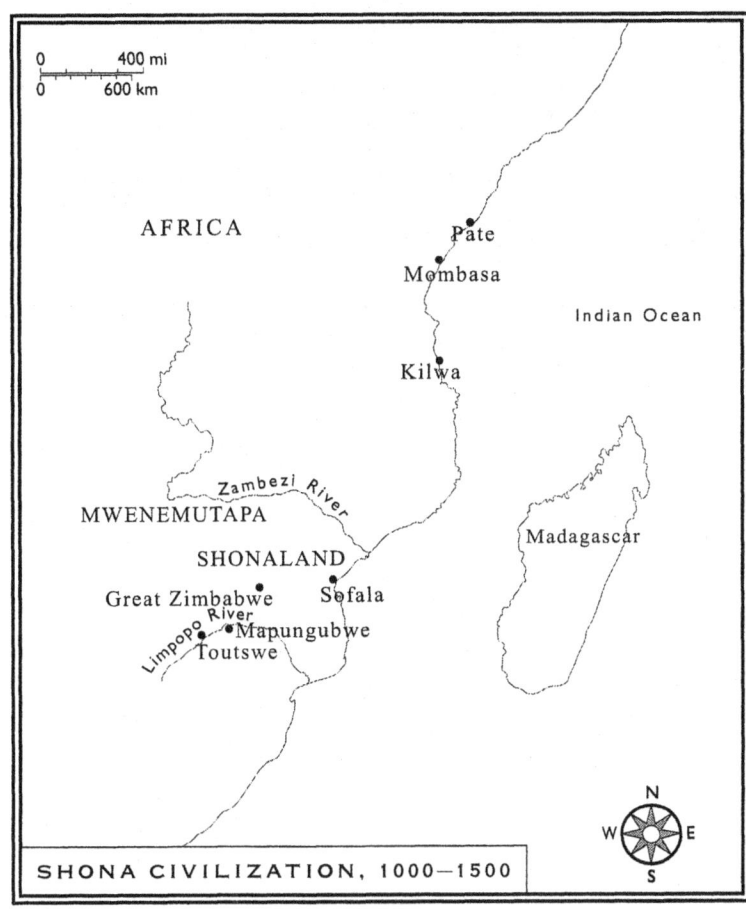

1. Which two cities were gold-exporting cities between 1100 and 1300?

   _____

   Draw a square around each of these cities.

2. What is the name of the city where the great stone buildings were found?

   _____

   Draw a circle around this city.

3. Draw a line along the path of the Portuguese as they claimed all the wealth for themselves in the 1600s.

CHAPTER 12 BLM   AFRICAN & MIDDLE EASTERN WORLD, 600–1500   **95**

PRIMARY SOURCES

Directions

With a partner, read the hymn to the god Mwari below. Then answer the questions that follow.

> Great Spirit!
> Piler up of rocks into towering mountains!
> When thou stampest on the stone,
> The dust rises and fills the land.
> Hardness of the precipice;
> Waters of the pool that turn
> Into misty rain when stirred.
> Vessel overflowing with oil! . . .
> Who seweth the heavens like cloth:
> Let him knit together that which is below.
> Caller forth of the branching trees.
> Thou bringest forth the shoots
> That they stand erect.
>
> Thou has filled the land with mankind,
> The dust rises on high, oh Lord!
> Wonderful One, thou livest
> In the midst of the sheltering rocks,
> Thou givest of rain to mankind:
> We pray to thee.
> Hear us, Lord!
> Show mercy when we beseech thee, Lord.
> Thou art on high with the spirits of the great.
> Thou raisest the grass-covered hills
> Above the earth, and createst,
> Gracious One.

1. For what is the god Mwari responsible? Name two things.

2. To what does the hymn singer compare Mwari's creation of the heavens?

3. Where can the god Mwari be found?

4. What are three names the hymn singer has for Mwari?

5. In a few sentences, describe the relationship between the hymn singer and Mwari.

CHAPTER TEST 12

THE AFRICAN & MIDDLE EASTERN WORLD, 600–1500

NAME _____ **DATE** _____

A. MULTIPLE CHOICE

Circle the letter of the best answer to each question.

1. How did changing from farming to raising cattle change the lives of the Bantu people?
   a. They became wealthy because they used the cattle as money.
   b. They grew poor and had to leave their homes.
   c. Their lives became very easy because they did not need much land.
   d. Their lives did not change.

2. What began happening at the same time gold began playing a bigger part in the costaal trade?
   a. The Bantu began building bigger houses.
   b. The Shona people began building a city of stone.
   c. The regions to the west of the plateau began producing gold.
   d. The regions to the west of the plateau became very poor.

3. What is the meaning of Zimbabwe?
   a. broken walls
   b. golden city
   c. city of legends
   d. stone buildings

4. All of the following are possible reasons that Great Zimbabwe was abandoned **except**
   a. the region became overpopulated and the environment could not support the people.
   b. the stone walls fell and the people were forced to move away.
   c. there was a shortage of salt and the king left it to conquer another city.
   d. gold was discovered in the northern part of the Shona plateau and miners moved there.

5. The Mwenemutapa kingdom came to be by all of these ways **except**
   a. the Portuguese took over the area.
   b. Matope extended the capital and opened trade with the coast.
   c. the king of Great Zimbabwe extended power over the Shona people.
   d. a powerful state called Karanga was established.

B. SHORT ANSWER

Write one or two sentences to answer each question.

6. How do archaeologists know that the trade brought wealth to rulers of Mapungubwe?

_____
_____
_____

7. Explain how Great Zimbabwe became wealthy.

_____
_____
_____

C. ESSAY

In an essay, describe the growth of trade in southeastern Africa between 1100 and 1400 and explain how trade influenced the lives of the Shona people. Support your essay with details from the chapter.

CHAPTER 13

THE EMPEROR'S GIRAFFE: EAST AFRICA'S SWAHILI COAST
(PAGES 148–158)

FOR HOMEWORK

STUDENT STUDY GUIDE pages 59–62

CHAPTER SUMMARY

The Swahili people of East Africa, many of whom were Muslim, descended from the Bantu of West Africa. The period from 1200 to 1500 is considered the golden age of Swahili civilization, in part because the Swahili had become involved in the far-reaching Muslim trade network. Swahili civilization was organized into competing city-states. Kilwa, which was abandoned in the 16th century, was the most prosperous and powerful because it controlled the gold trade. Many Swahili towns still survive.

PERFORMANCE OBJECTIVES

- To compare Swahili origin myths with the actual origin of Swahili
- To analyze trade patterns of the Swahili
- To describe the "golden age" of the Swahili, including advances and daily life

BUILDING BACKGROUND

Have students discuss trade as it is practiced in the world today. Ask them to identify the sources of some important raw materials such as oil and challenge them to identify leading exports of the United States and other countries. Make sure students consider the ease and fluidity of trade today. To illustrate, have them look at clothing, food, electronic and other household items to see where they come from. Encourage students to compare and contrast contemporary trade with what they learn of trade between the Swahili of East Africa and traders from Persia, India, and Arabia many centuries ago.

CAST OF CHARACTERS

Hasan (hah-SAHN) **bin Sulayman** (soo-lay-MAHN) king of Kilwa

VOCABULARY

infidel nonbeliever in Christianity or Islam

migrated moved from one place to settle somewhere else

prestigious having high standing among others

dynasty a series of rulers from the same family

quay a wharf or bank where ships are loaded and unloaded

As needed, have students consult the glossary to define the following words: *Arabic, Bantu, caliphs, clan, Islam, Muslims, Quran, Shiite*.

WORKING WITH PRIMARY SOURCES

Most of the written descriptions we have of the cities on the eastern coast of Africa are based on eyewitness accounts written down by European and Islamic visitors to the region. These reports are inevitably influenced by the opinions and attitudes of the foreigners who gave them. Discuss with the class the challenge of giving a truly objective description of a culture that may at first seem strange and exotic. Read aloud the account by Portuguese writer João de Barros on page 151 and ask them which passages might not be entirely trustworthy.

GEOGRAPHY CONNECTION

Location Distribute the blackline master of the map for this chapter, African Trade 700–1500. Have students identify the Swahili cities on the map and estimate the distance between the West African coast and East African Swahili cities.

READING COMPREHENSION QUESTIONS

1. According to one story, what was the price the Persians paid for Kilwa and how did they pay it? *(They had to circle the island with colored clothes.)*
2. How do experts know that the Swahili-speaking people of East Africa descend from Bantu speakers of West Africa? *(The Swahili language is a Bantu language.)*
3. What was the basis of a Muslim Swahili child's education? *(the Quran)*
4. Over what did the Swahili city-states compete? *(trade, alliances, control of farmlands)*
5. Why and when was Kilwa abandoned? *(It was abandoned because of Portuguese attacks in the 16th century)*

CRITICAL THINKING QUESTIONS

1. Why was life so much better for the Swahili during the 14th through 16th centuries than it had been for their ancestors before 1000 CE? *(The early ancestors had migrated from West Africa and had to learn how to survive and thrive in a new place. They had to learn by trial and error to survive in a marine environment with different sources of food, building materials, and trade items.)*
2. How resourceful do you think the early Swahili were? Why do you think so? *(Possible answer: They were very resourceful. They learned how to make iron and beads from seashells to trade.)*
3. Would you have wanted to live in Kilwa during the 15th century? Give reasons for your answer. *(Answers will vary.)*

SOCIAL SCIENCES

Civics Have students choose to take on the role of either a Swahili Muslim boy or a Swahili Muslim girl and write a diary entry that describes a typical day in their lives. Remind them to use details from the chapter. When they are done, have them read their entries aloud and compare how boys' lives and girls' lives were different.

THEN and NOW

In the Middle Ages Kilwa was one of the world's great trading centers, a beautiful and thriving city-state. Now it is an intriguing ruin in Tanzania that was designated a World Heritage Site by UNESCO in 1981.

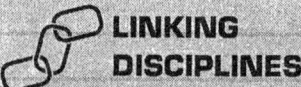

LINKING DISCIPLINES

Science Monsoons greatly influenced trade between Arabia, the Persian Gulf, and India and the Swahili cities of East Africa. Have students research monsoons to find out what they are, how they are formed, and what effect they had on navigation of sailing ships during medieval times.

LITERACY TIPS

In addition to using the suggestions in the Supporting Learning and Extending Learning sections, refer back frequently to pages 16–19 for strategies and advice from a literacy coach.

READING AND LANGUAGE ARTS

Reading Nonfiction Ask students to reread the quotations in the chapter. For each quotation, have them answer the following questions. What is the author's attitude toward the subject? How can you tell?

Using Language Discuss with students the ways in which an author's choice of words can signal bias. Write the word *infidel* on the board, and point out that this word appears several times in the first quotation. Explain that infidel means someone who does not believe in a religion such as Islam or Christianity. The meaning, or denotation, is straightforward, but the connotation is negative. Let students find other words in the chapter whose connotations are positive or negative and thus hint at the author's feelings toward the subject.

WRITING

Expository Sentences Ask students to describe an aspect of the city-state of Kilwa. They might choose the sultan's palace or the house of an ordinary person. Other possible topics include the quay where goods are loaded and unloaded from ships and the view of the city from a distance.

SUPPORTING LEARNING

English Language Learners The syntax and vocabulary of the quotations in this chapter may challenge English language learners. List archaic and uncommon words and the names of people and places from the quotations on the board. Pronounce and define the words. Then read each quotation aloud.

Struggling Readers Ask students to work in pairs to use the outline graphic organizer (see reproducibles at the back of this guide) to summarize the rise and fall of Kilwa, as well as any other parts of the chapter that they find confusing. Provide assistance as necessary.

EXTENDING LEARNING

Enrichment Encourage students to learn more about the religious beliefs and cultural practices of the Islamic Swahili, their imports and exports, or the building styles and materials they used during the "golden age." Ask pairs or small groups of students to research the area that interests them most and present their findings to the class.

Extension Let interested students make a mural that shows their vision of Kilwa in 1498 based on the descriptions and illustrations in the chapter. Encourage them to combine factual information with their imagination to produce unique artworks.

AFRICAN TRADE, 700–1500

Directions

Use the map to answer the questions.

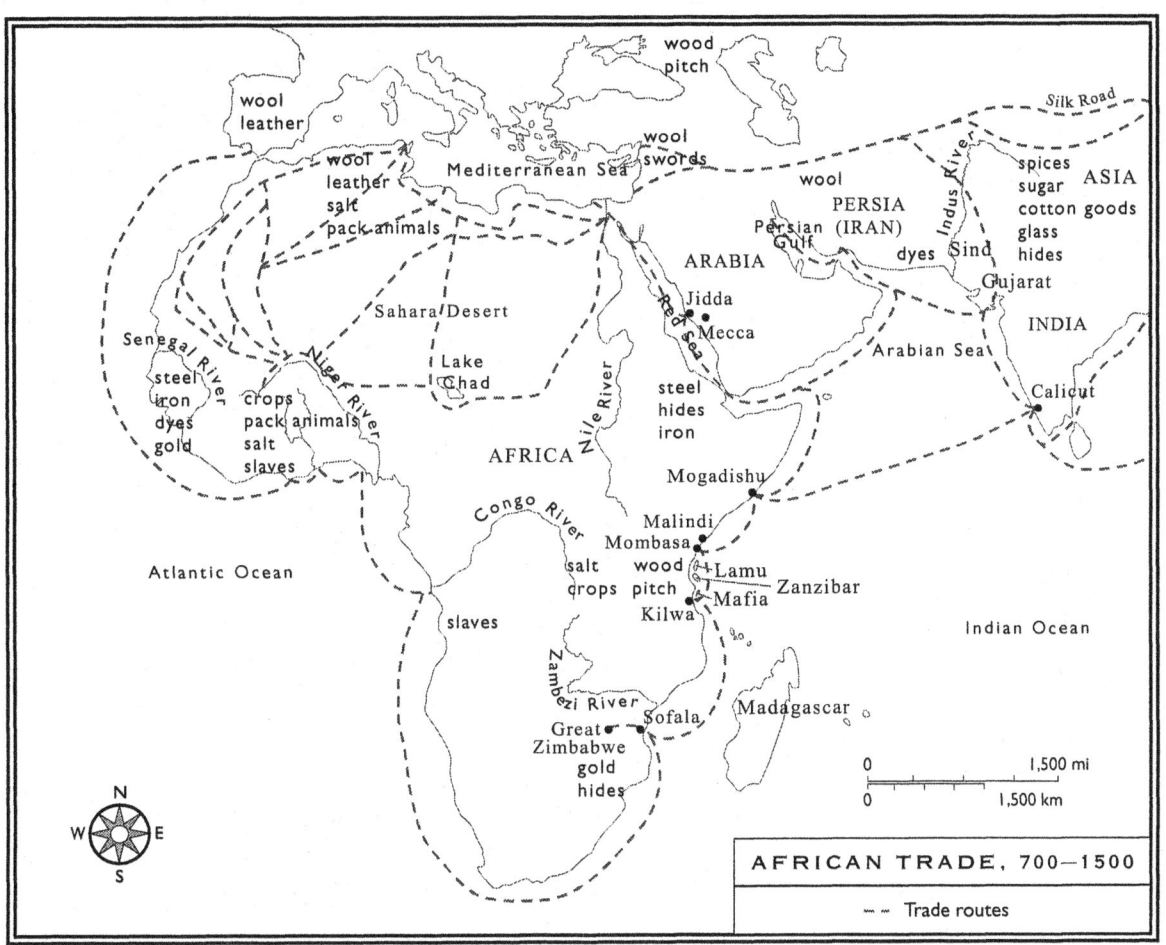

1. Which trade items come from two or more places; which come from a single place?

_____
_____
_____

2. How did the main trading "highways" of Southern Africa differ from those of Northern Africa?

_____
_____
_____

3. What is similar about the location of most of the cities on the map? Why do you think this is?

_____
_____
_____

PRIMARY SOURCES

Directions

Read the excerpts and answer the questions that follow. The first is from Ibn Battuta's *Travels in Asia and Africa 1325–1354*. The second is from the epic poem *The Lusíads* by Luiz Vaz de Camões, which celebrates Vasco da Gama's voyages to Africa and India in the 15th century.

I. We came to Mambasa [Mombasa], a large island two days' journey by sea from the Swahili country. It possesses no territory on the mainland. They have fruit trees on the island, but no cereals, which have to be brought to them from the Swahili. Their food consists chiefly of bananas and fish.

II. There could be seen a magnificent
City with many noble edifices
Marking the whole curve of the bay,
A landmark visible for many miles,
And ruled by a king of great antiquity;
Mombasa it is named, both isle and city.

1. What is the likely reason that the people of Mombasa did not grow cereal (grain)?

2. What evidence proves to Ibn Battuta that the people were pious?

3. What does the Portuguese poet de Camões mean when he writes that Mombasa is "both isle and city"?

4. What word best describes de Camões's impression of Mombasa?

CHAPTER TEST 13
THE AFRICAN & MIDDLE EASTERN WORLD, 600–1500

NAME   **DATE**

A. MULTIPLE CHOICE

Circle the letter of the best answer to each question.

1. Between the late 700s and 1200, what happened to the Islamic population of East Africa?
   - **a.** It disappeared.
   - **b.** It grew.
   - **c.** It decreased.
   - **d.** It stayed the same.

2. Which material was used to build houses in Kliwa?
   - **a.** sand
   - **b.** coral
   - **c.** stone
   - **d.** shells

3. What was a shamba?
   - **a.** a school
   - **b.** a store
   - **c.** a palace
   - **d.** a farm

4. Which occupation would a boy from Kilwa be unlikely to follow?
   - **a.** artist
   - **b.** trader
   - **c.** fisherman
   - **d.** farmer

5. When was the golden age of Swahili civilization?
   - **a.** 350–650
   - **b.** 1000–1200
   - **c.** 1200–1500
   - **d.** 1600–1800

B. SHORT ANSWER

Write several sentences to answer the question below.

Husuni Kubwa, the home of the sultan of Kilwa, was probably the grandest building in sub-Saharan Africa. What did it look like?

_____
_____
_____
_____
_____
_____
_____

C. ESSAY

Why is the period from 1200 to 1500 is considered the golden age of Swahili civilization? Write an essay to answer this question that includes details from the chapter of trade, everyday life and religion.

The African & Middle Eastern World, 600–1500

NAME _____ **DATE** _____

Directions
Answer each of the following questions. Use additional paper if necessary

1. Write a paragraph explaining how the city of Mecca changed between the 6th and 7th centuries.

2. Write one or two paragraphs comparing the lives of the Bedouin and the Berbers. Explain how they were alike and how they were different.

3. Write a paragraph explaining the steps of the spread of Islam throughout the Middle East and Africa.

4. The Muslim faith guided the people of the Middle East. Write one or two paragraphs explaining the Muslim beliefs and teachings that led the Muslims to spread Islam.

5. The ulamas and the Mutazilites disagreed about Islamic religious teaching. In one or two paragraphs, explain what each side thought.

6. Muhammad said, "The search for knowledge is a sacred duty imposed upon every Muslim." Write one or two paragraphs explaining how this statement was lived out in Baghdad after the House of Wisdom was established. Mention the contributions of at least three people.

7. Conquering the city of Constantinople had been a goal of the Ottomans. Write a paragraph explaining how the Ottomans finally managed to take Constantinople as part of their empire.

8. Write one or two paragraphs comparing how at least two of the African kings were treated by their subjects. Explain what this says about the relationship between the kings and their subjects.

9. Write one or two paragraphs explaining how the gold trade impacted the religious lives of the people of western Sudan in the 13th century.

10. Write a paragraph explaining the trade system on the Swahili coast.

SCORING RUBRIC

The reproducibles on the following pages have been adapted from this rubric for use as handouts and a student self-scoring activity, with added focus on planning, cooperation, revision and presentation. You may wish to tailor the self-scoring activity—for example, asking students to comment on how low scores could be improved, or focusing only on specific rubric points. Use the Library/Media Center Research Log to help students focus and evaluate their research for projects and assignments.

As with any rubric, you should introduce and explain the rubric before students begin their assignments. The more thoroughly your students understand how they will be evaluated, the better prepared they will be to produce projects that fulfill your expectations.

	ORGANIZATION	CONTENT	ORAL/WRITTEN CONVENTIONS	GROUP PARTICIPATION
4	• Clearly addresses all parts of the writing task. • Demonstrates a clear understanding of purpose and audience. • Maintains a consistent point of view, focus, and organizational structure, including the effective use of transitions. • Includes a clearly presented central idea with relevant facts, details, and/or explanations.	• Demonstrates that the topic was well researched. • Uses only information that was essential and relevant to the topic. • Presents the topic thoroughly and accurately. • Reaches reasonable conclusions clearly based on evidence.	• Contains few, if any, errors in grammar, punctuation, capitalization, or spelling. • Uses a variety of sentence types. • Speaks clearly, using effective volume and intonation.	• Demonstrated high levels of participation and effective decision making. • Planned well and used time efficiently. • Demonstrated ability to negotiate opinions fairly and reach compromise when needed. • Utilized effective visual aids.
3	• Addresses all parts of the writing task. • Demonstrates a general understanding of purpose and audience. • Maintains a mostly consistent point of view, focus, and organizational structure, including the effective use of some transitions. • Presents a central idea with mostly relevant facts, details, and/or explanations.	• Demonstrates that the topic was sufficiently researched. • Uses mainly information that was essential and relevant to the topic. • Presents the topic accurately but leaves some aspects unexplored. • Reaches reasonable conclusions loosely related to evidence.	• Contains some errors in grammar, punctuation, capitalization, or spelling. • Uses a variety of sentence types. • Speaks somewhat clearly, using effective volume and intonation.	• Demonstrated good participation and decision making with few distractions. • Planning and used its time acceptably. • Demonstrated ability to negotiate opinions and compromise with little aggression or unfairness.
2	• Addresses only parts of the writing task. • Demonstrates little understanding of purpose and audience. • Maintains an inconsistent point of view, focus, and/or organizational structure, which may include ineffective or awkward transitions that do not unify important ideas. • Suggests a central idea with limited facts, details, and/or explanations.	• Demonstrates that the topic was minimally researched. • Uses a mix of relevant and irrelevant information. • Presents the topic with some factual errors and leaves some aspects unexplored. • Reaches conclusions that do not stem from evidence presented in the project.	• Contains several errors in grammar, punctuation, capitalization, or spelling. These errors may interfere with the reader's understanding of the writing. • Uses little variety in sentence types. • Speaks unclearly or too quickly. May interfere with the audience's understanding of the project.	• Demonstrated uneven participation or was often off-topic. Task distribution was lopsided. • Did not show a clear plan for the project, and did not use time well. • Allowed one or two opinions to dominate the activity, or had trouble reaching a fair consensus.
1	• Addresses only one part of the writing task. • Demonstrates no understanding of purpose and audience. • Lacks a point of view, focus, organizational structure, and transitions that unify important ideas. • Lacks a central idea but may contain marginally related facts, details, and/or explanations.	• Demonstrates that the topic was poorly researched. • Does not discriminate relevant from irrelevant information. • Presents the topic incompletely, with many factual errors. • Did not reach conclusions.	• Contains serious errors in grammar, punctuation, capitalization, or spelling. These errors interfere with the reader's understanding of the writing. • Uses no sentence variety. • Speaks unclearly. The audience must struggle to understand the project.	• Demonstrated poor participation by the majority of the group. Tasks were completed by a small minority. • Failed to show planning or effective use of time. • Was dominated by a single voice, or allowed hostility to derail the project.

NAME _____ **PROJECT** _____

DATE _____

ORGANIZATION & FOCUS	CONTENT	ORAL/WRITTEN CONVENTIONS	GROUP PARTICIPATION
☐	☐	☐	☐

COMMENTS AND SUGGESTIONS

UNDERSTANDING YOUR SCORE

Organization: Your project should be clear, focused on a main idea, and organized. You should use details and facts to support your main idea.

Content: You should use strong research skills. Your project should be thorough and accurate.

Oral/Written Conventions: For writing projects, you should use good composition, grammar, punctuation, and spelling, with a good variety of sentence types. For oral projects, you should engage the class using good public speaking skills.

Group Participation: Your group should cooperate fairly and use its time well to plan, assign and revise the tasks involved in the project.

NAME _____ GROUP MEMBERS _____

_____
_____
_____

Use this worksheet to describe your project by finishing the sentences below.
For individual projects and writing assignments, use the "How I did" section.
For group projects, use both "How I did" and "How we did" sections.

The purpose of this project is to :

Scoring Key =   4 – extremely well
                3 – well
                2 – could have been better
                1 – not well at all

HOW I DID

I understood the purpose and requirements for this project…

I planned and organized my time and work…

This project showed clear organization that emphasized the central idea…

I supported my point with details and description…

I polished and revised this project…

I utilized correct grammar and good writing/speaking style…

Overall, this project met its purpose…

HOW WE DID

We divided up tasks…

We cooperated and listened to each other…

We talked through what we didn't understand…

We used all our time to make this project the best it could be…

Overall, as a group we worked together…

I contributed and cooperated with the team…

NAME _____

LIBRARY/ MEDIA CENTER RESEARCH LOG

DUE DATE _____

What I Need to Find

Brainstorm: Other Sources and Places to Look

Places I **Know** to Look

I need to use:
☐ primary sources.
☐ secondary

WHAT I FOUND

Title/Author/Location (call # or URL)

_____

_____

_____

_____

_____

_____

	Book/Periodical	Website	Other		Primary Source	Secondary Source		Suggestion	Library Catalog	Browsing	Internet Search	Web link		helpful	relevant
	☐	☐	☐		☐	☐	**How I Found it**	☐	☐	☐	☐	☐	**Rate each source from 1 (low) to 4 (high) in the categories below**	___	___
	☐	☐	☐		☐	☐		☐	☐	☐	☐	☐		___	___
	☐	☐	☐		☐	☐		☐	☐	☐	☐	☐		___	___
	☐	☐	☐		☐	☐		☐	☐	☐	☐	☐		___	___
	☐	☐	☐		☐	☐		☐	☐	☐	☐	☐		___	___
	☐	☐	☐		☐	☐		☐	☐	☐	☐	☐		___	___

GRAPHIC ORGANIZERS

GUIDELINES

Reproducibles of seven different graphic organizers are provided on the following pages. These give your students a variety of ways to sort and order all the information they are receiving in this course. Use the organizers for homework assignments, classroom activities, tests, small group projects, and as ways to help the students take notes as they read.

1. Determine which graphic organizers work best for the content you are teaching. Some are useful for identifying main ideas and details; others work better for making comparisons, and so on.

2. Graphic organizers help students focus on the central points of the lesson while leaving out irrelevant details.

3. Use graphic organizers to give a visual picture of the key ideas you are teaching.

4. Graphic organizers can help students recall important information. Suggest students use them to study for tests.

5. Graphic organizers provide a visual way to show the connections between different content areas.

6. Graphic organizers can enliven traditional lesson plans and encourage greater interactivity within the classroom.

7. Apply graphic organizers to give students a concise, visual way to break down complex ideas.

8. Encourage students to use graphic organizers to identify patterns and clarify their ideas.

9. Graphic organizers stimulate creative thinking in the classroom, in small groups, and for the individual student.

10. Help students determine which graphic organizers work best for their purposes, and encourage them to use graphic organizers collaboratively whenever they can.

11. Help students customize graphic organizers as particular exercises dictate: e.g., more or fewer boxes, lines, or blanks than appear.

OUTLINE

MAIN IDEA: _____
_____
_____

    DETAIL: _____
    _____

    DETAIL: _____
    _____

    DETAIL: _____
    _____

MAIN IDEA: _____
_____
_____

    DETAIL: _____
    _____

    DETAIL: _____
    _____

    DETAIL: _____
    _____

Name _____   Date _____

MAIN IDEA MAP

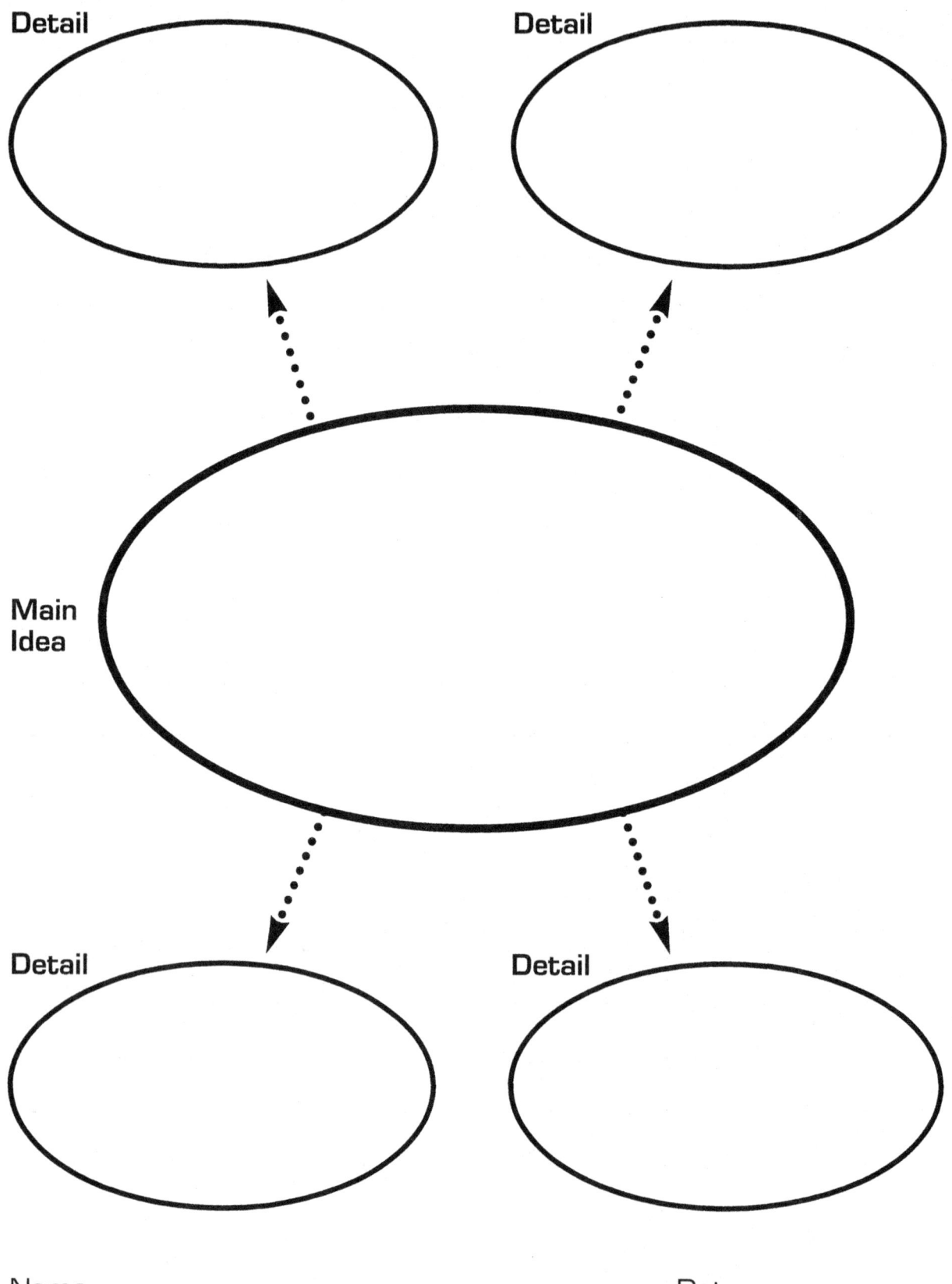

Name _____ Date _____

K-W-L CHART

K	W	L
What I Know	What I Want to Know	What I Learned

Name _____   Date _____

VENN DIAGRAM

Write differences in the circles. Write similarities where the circles overlap.

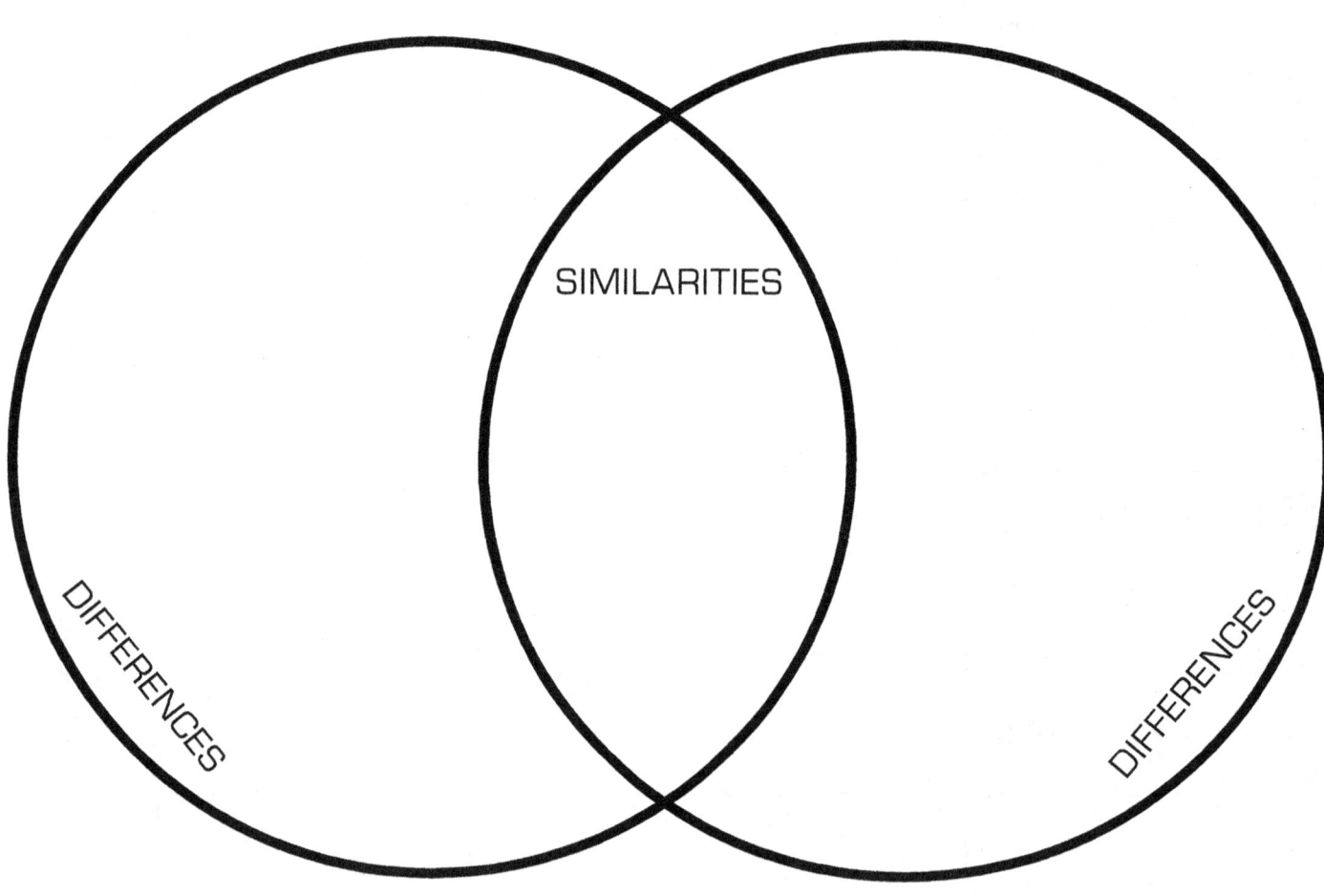

Name _____ Date _____

TIMELINE

DATE

EVENT Draw lines to connect the event to the correct year on the timeline.

Name _____ Date

SEQUENCE OF EVENTS CHART

Event

Next Event

Next Event

Next Event

Next Event

Name _____ Date _____

T-CHART

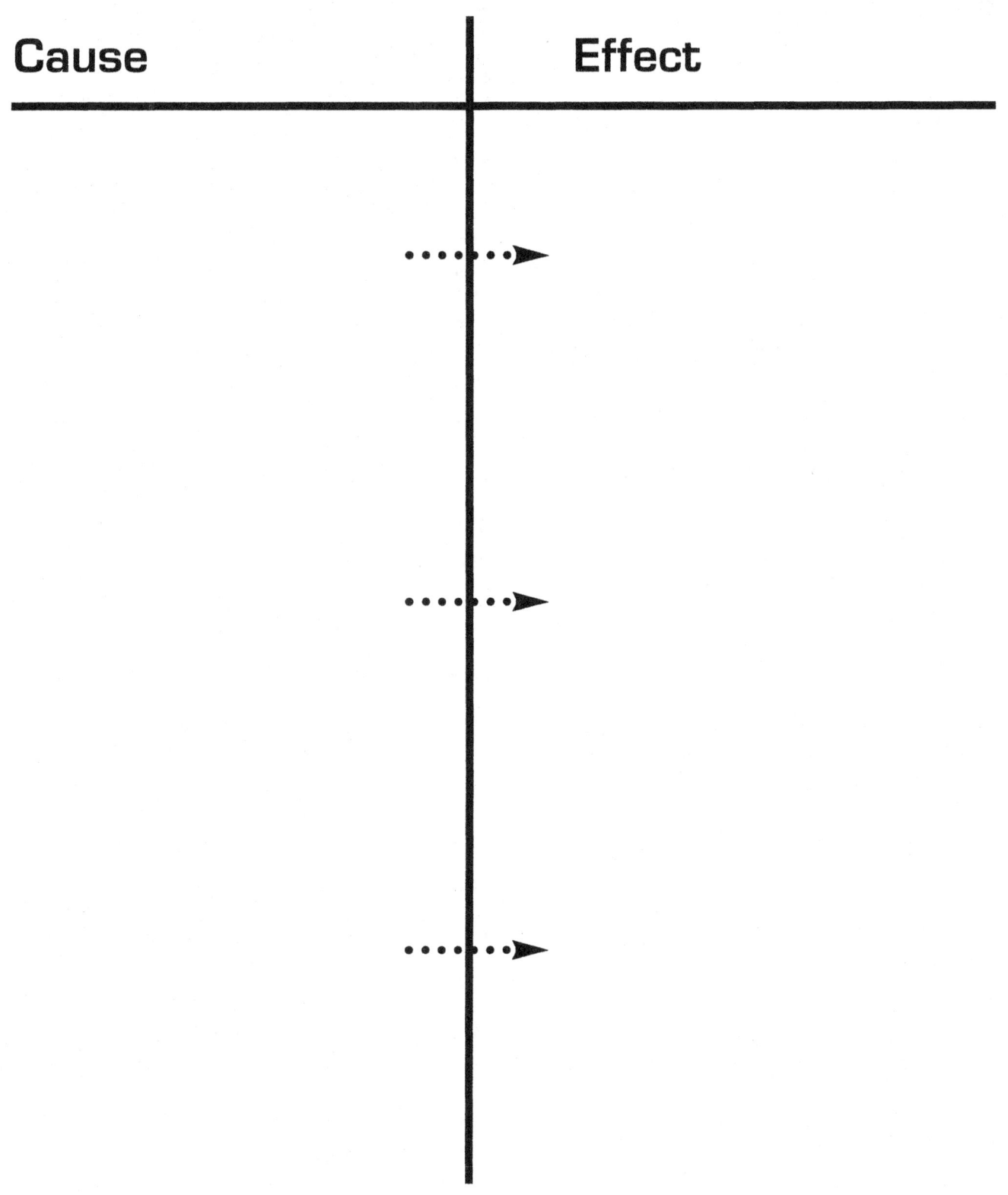

Name _____ Date _____

ANSWER KEY

CHAPTER 1

BLACKLINE MASTER 1

1. Symbol should appear at Mecca.
2. Symbol for wheat should appear at Yemen.
3. Symbol should appear just north of Mecca.

BLACKLINE MASTER 2

1. These lines reflect the nomadic nature of the Bedouin since they reference camels, the common mode of transportation for the Bedouin.
2. The poem's placement on the wall of the Ka'ba gives it a sacred or religious significance.
3. The narrator of the poem dictates commands and speaks with authority. For example, he says, "Drive him on!"
4. Answers will vary.

CHAPTER TEST

A. 1. a; 2. b; 3. d; 4. b; 5. c

B. 6. The Quraysh tribe convinced the Bedouin to allow safe passage for people to visit the sacred shrine of the Ka'ba for one month; this month is called Ramadan.

7. 6th-century Arabia was home to a great number of diverse religions: Jews, Christians, tribes believing in many gods but considering Allah as the chief god (e.g., the Quraysh), tribes worshipping goddesses, etc.

C. *Possible points:* the Bedouin are democratic; tribal elders meet to decide and argue policy; every tribe has a shaykh who negotiates agreements with other tribes and settles disputes among tribal elders.

CHAPTER 2

BLACKLINE MASTER 1

1. Arrows should point from Axum east to the tip of Yemen, then through Yemen northwest to Mecca; East and northwest.
2. The Red Sea
3. Badr
4. Medina
5. Mecca

BLACKLINE MASTER 2

1. When Muhammad preached that there was only God, the Arabs questioned if Muhammad was designating that one God himself.
2. They might have felt threatened because they believed in idols and Muhammad's message was very unfamiliar.
3. Polytheism is belief in more than one god. Monotheism is belief in only one god. This text shows that when Muhammad spoke about just one god, the Arabs thought it was strange because they worshipped many idols.

CHAPTER TEST

A. 1. b; 2. a; 3. c; 4. c; 5. a; 6. c

B. 7. Muhammad was troubled by the differences he saw between rich and poor, and would spend hours in meditation and prayer. When he was 40, according to his biographer, "God honored him with his mission . . . Gabriel brought him the command of God." At first he was badly frightened by the moments of revelation, but then he began by converting his family and friends.

8. These are the basic duties that all Muslims must practice. They include giving witness to one God and to Muhammad as the messenger of God; praying five times a day; giving alms to the needy; fasting during Ramadan; and making the pilgrimage to Mecca at least once in one's life.

C. Answers might include Muhammad's visit by the angel Gabriel; his marriage to Khadija; his preaching the message of God; his establishment of Medina; the battles at Badr and Uhud; leading his followers to Mecca; destroying the idols and statues in the Ka'ba; Muhammad's laying out of the Five Pillars; Muhammad's death.

CHAPTER 3

BLACKLINE MASTER 1

1. About 2,800 miles/4,500 km east and about 1,600 miles/2,700 km west
2. Shading should include the Arabian Peninsula.
3. Shading should include the rest of the original shaded area.
4. Constantinople was separated from major portions of the Muslim area by the Mediterranean Sea.

BLACKLINE MASTER 2

1. To his army of men preparing to attack the Spaniards.
2. He is risking his life as much as the rest of the men. He will die fighting with his men or he will live on to continue the fight in their name.
3. God
4. That the word of God be spread into Spain and that Islam becomes the religion there.

CHAPTER TEST

A. 1. a; 2. c; 3. c; 4. a; 5. c

B. 6. Muslims believed it was their religious duty to extend Islamic rule. They also believed that fighting in a holy war, guaranteed them a place in heaven.

7. Umar divided the Muslims into two armies: one pressed north into Byzantine territory and the other was sent northeast into lands held by the Sassanids. He caught both off guard and therefore gained control.

C. *Possible points:* similarities—both tended to be nomadic and live off the livestock that traveled with them; differences—Bedouin wore long gowns, while the Berbers wore little clothing; the Berbers eventually accepted Islam.

CHAPTER 4

BLACKLINE MASTER 1

1. Siffin
2. Damascus
3. Karbala

BLACKLINE MASTER 2

1. To fill his saddlebag with silver and gold.
2. Because he wants to be rewarded for killing Muhammad's grandson.
3. Al-Husayn is described as being of noblest parents of the best descent. He means that al-Husayn comes from the lineage of Muhammad.
4. The person is upset to see the mouth of this man, who was kissed by his grandfather Muhammad, defiled.
5. This event, more than any other, hardened Shiite feelings against the caliphs and the Muslim majority who supported them. Husayn is still considered a martyr by Shiites today, who hold his tomb to be sacred.

CHAPTER TEST

A. 1. d; 2. b; 3. c; 4. a; 5. c

B. 6. Positive: Uthman brought skilled administrators to manage the large Muslim empire; Negative: Uthman's clan, the Umayyads, had been opponents of Muhammad at Mecca; Uthman used favoritism to give the highest positions to his Umayyad relatives.

C. Details from chapter should flesh out the following main ideas: Shiites believed Muhammad had chosen Ali as his successor, so they opposed the Umayyad; Mawalis were angry at being treated as second-class Muslims and having jizya collected from them; they joined forces in a Shiite rebellion that swept the Umayyads out of Damascus in 750 and established a new clan of caliphs.

CHAPTER 5

BLACKLINE MASTER 1

1. Baghdad
2. It is near the Tigris River, which helps in transportation, and it is in the geographic center of the empire.
3. Aden
4. The Port of Aden is at the southernmost tip of the country and surrounded by water, which makes it easily accessible by ship and closer to the lands surrounding the Indian Ocean.

ANSWER KEY

BLACKLINE MASTER 2

1. The custodian shows compassion to the slave; instead of beating or even scolding the slave, the custodian helps the slave buy a replacement dish. In this way, the custodian treats the slave as an equal and shows him respect, as described in the passage from the Quran.
2. The Quran suggests that slaves are worthy of respect and of being treated as equals, rather than simply as human possessions with no rights of their own. Also, a slave can have an important role in how the master participates in his religious practices.

CHAPTER TEST

A. 1. c; 2. a; 3. d; 4. d; 5. c
B. 6. Trade enabled the Abbasid caliphate to spread its influence and power. Their extensive trade network helped to unite the extensive empire.
7. Both the Kharijite and Shiite movements attracted Muslims who opposed the hereditary control of the caliphate by just one family. And the Shiites believed that Muslims should only be led by direct descendents of Fatima, Muhammad's daughter.
C. *Possible points:* developments under the Abbasid caliphate—new government with its capital in Baghdad; royal post office; spy network; teams of translators to help communication between lands; provinces and their respective governors established; growth of religious scholarship; extensive trade network; craft guilds for craftspeople; Quran schools. Despite these developments, the Abbasids were eventually weakened by slave, Kharijite, and Shiite revolts.

CHAPTER 6
BLACKLINE MASTER 1

1. Answers will vary, but should include the following: the Quran is God's divine word as revealed to Muhammad and stresses moral principles and guidelines about piety and justice. The Sunna is the living example of Muhammad and provides guidance about ordinary life. The Sunna was developed after Muhammad's death from *hadith,* or accounts of the things Muhammad had said and done, repeated by his companions. Students might also include details about the origin of the Quran or examples of the Sunna's guidance for daily life.

BLACKLINE MASTER 2

1. God
2. Answers will vary but may include that through becoming Love's slave, one will find freedom.
3. A bird hatching from an egg.
4. Answers will vary.

CHAPTER TEST

A. 1. a; 2. c; 3. d; 4. b; 5. b
B. Answers will vary.
C. *Possible answers:* the Quran does not provide detailed instructions about ordinary life. In looking for guidance in being good Muslims, Muhammad's companions repeated *hadith,* or accounts of the things Muhammad had said and done. These form the basis of the Sunna, which is the living example of Muhammad in contrast to the Quran, which is God's divine word. The Sunna contains *hadith* such as how Muslims should greet each other, etc.

CHAPTER 7
BLACKLINE MASTER 1

1. Baghdad
2. Baghdad
3. Qayrawan and Fez
4. Seville and Cordoba
5. Tangier
6. Granada

BLACKLINE MASTER 2

1. The doe treated him as if she were his mother.
2. He imitated their calls and went out to forage and graze.
3. They were used to each other and the child lived like them so he seemed to be one of them.

CHAPTER TEST

A. 1. b; 2. d; 3. a; 4. a; 5. c
B. 6. He wrote about his studies of the nature of light, optics, and the eye, which were later translated into Latin, making his work accessible to scientists in other countries.
7. A *rilha* is a voyage undertaken for religious and educational purposes. Ibn Battuta spent his life traveling throughout and beyond the Islamic world for these purposes.
C. *Possible points:* Ibn Battuta's 14th-century travelogue was widely read; the Abbasid court poets created the poetic form *abad*; the collection of stories *The Thousand and One Nights*; the poetry collection the *Rubaiyat*; Edward Fitzgerald translated some of Omar Khayyám's poetry for a western audience; British novelist Daniel Defoe was influenced by Ibn Tufayl's work *Alive, Son of Awake*.

CHAPTER 8
BLACKLINE MASTER 1

1. Northern Syria
2. Bursa, Anatolia
3. Constantinople
4. Vienna

BLACKLINE MASTER 2

1. The Seljuk Turks were tireless warriors whose horses tired before they did. They were also excellent marksmen who could easily hit their targets.
2. Answers will vary.
3. Both are tireless and excellent warriors.
4. The Turks use arrows to kill the enemy from a distance. The Ottomans collected the enemies into a ditch and killed them there.

CHAPTER TEST

A. 1. d; 2. b; 3. c; 4. d; 5. a
B. 6. By giving each commander his own state, Orhan ensured the loyalty of these men to his sultanate.
7. The Ottoman armies were able to put down any resistance and expand the Ottoman Empire.
C. *Answers may include:* Suleyman extended Ottoman holdings into Tunis, Algiers, Rhodes, and most of the lands bordering the Mediterranean. He seized control of Baghdad and Basra from Shiite forces. He supported religious scholars and enforced Islamic rule; arranged for an annual pilgrimage to Mecca; and built mosques. But one of his wives convinced him his favored son was plotting against him, so he strangled him.

CHAPTER 9
BLACKLINE MASTER 1

1. Sahara Desert
2. Sahel
3. Ghana
4. Qayrawan
5. It is mostly a region of desert and grasslands; therefore, its inhabitants led hard lives as farmers (when possible) or as caravan traders, who were forced to travel long distances in dangerous conditions.

BLACKLINE MASTER 2

1. steadfast, brave, light-footed, tough
2. good camel drivers, know the conditions and forms of the land well and how to find their way over it, can be guided to water points, have a sense of direction
3. Berbers are nomadic people. If the Berbers can find water and move around the desert easily, they will stay safe and healthy longer.
4. Answers will vary, but students might surmise that the Berbers would not have survived *without* a good sense of direction in the desert, with its constantly shifting sands and harsh conditions. They would have needed to perfect their ability to notice landmarks and to read natural clues, such as wind direction and position of moon, sun, and stars. This knowledge would have been passed down from parents to children and highly valued in the tribe.

ANSWER KEY

CHAPTER TEST

A. 1. b; **2.** d; **3.** a; **4.** b; **5.** c

B. 6. Ghana was located between the gold fields and the saltworks.

7. West African towns were able to prosper and gain previously inaccessible goods, such as: dates, copper, horses, cloth, and weapons. The wealth trade brought to the towns helped them grow into cities and then kingdoms.

C. *Possible points:* Abdallah ibn Yasin established a *ribat* in order to influence Muslims to adhere to strict Sunni Islamic principles. When these methods of conversion failed, Ibn Yasin resorted to force and declared a *jihad*. This Almoravid jihad stifled Shiite and Kharijite Islam, and Sunni Islam became the accepted form of Islam throughout North and West Africa after the 11th century.

CHAPTER 10

BLACKLINE MASTER 1

1. Niani
2. Buré and Bitu
3. Timbuktu

BLACKLINE MASTER 2

1. A platform has been built and covered in silk and pillows and shade has been created out of silk.
2. *Possible answers:* dignified, serious, unhurried.
3. Great respect, as shown in the details of how he enters, the comparison to a preacher, and how he is treated as he enters.

CHAPTER TEST

A. 1. c; **2.** b; **3.** b; **4.** b; **5.** c

B. Sundiata, powerful chief of the Mande people who established the kingdom of Mali; Mansa Musa, king of Mali who was made famous by his many gifts of gold along his pilgrimage route to Mecca; Mansa Sulayman, king of Mali who, like Mansa Musa, upheld the Five Pillars of Islam and enforced Islamic law; Sonni Ali, great ruler of the Songhay dynasty who captured Timbuktu in 1468; Muhammad Turé, a general under Sonni Ali who seized power of the Songhay dynasty after Ali's death

C. Answers may include the following ideas: Mandinka people were farmers and believed the nature spirits and gods had power over what grew, and the mansas therefore continued traditions such as animal sacrifice. But they also went on pilgrimages to Mecca, and encouraged Islamic rituals and holidays, and had court officials enforce Islamic law and the Five Pillars of Islam. But some other Sudanese practices continued as well, such as allowing the Queen Mother power. In this way, mansas bridged the traditional culture and the new faith of Islam.

CHAPTER 11

BLACKLINE MASTER 1

1. The lines should go from Buré and Bitu to Ifé and then up the Niger River to Jenne. The distances are: Buré=approx. 2,000 miles/3,600 km and Bitu=approx. 1,600 miles/3,200 km.
2. Ifé was between the forest and the wooded grasslands and was close to the Niger River on which traders could transport goods.

BLACKLINE MASTER 2

1. *Possible answer:* Ifé was critically important to the Yoruba, who believed that the city was the source of life on the planet.
2. *Possible answer:* Readers might have found it interesting and poetic or misguided and ignorant, but they would have found it completely fanciful in either case.
3. *Possible answer:* He was skilled in many areas that kings usually are not.
4. *Possible answer:* The Bini had contact with outsiders, educated themselves, and were able to conduct war.

CHAPTER TEST

A. 1. d **2.** b **3.** b **4.** d **5.** b

B. 6. Oral tradition was the foundation for the beliefs of these people. For example, the Onis believed they were descendents of Oduduwa, the first man, who was the main character in a story they passed down through generations.

7. The bronzes often illustrated the divine status of Benin rulers. For example, one bronze depicts an Oba with the feet of crayfish, which symbolized the belief that the Oba could walk on water.

C. *Possible points:* Characteristics include the following: Ewuare: warlike, expansion-minded, brave, wise, talented, and so on; Oguola: interested in art, interested in commemorating his reign; both: divine rulers, powerful

CHAPTER 12

BLACKLINE MASTER 1

1. Sofala and Kilwa
2. Great Zimbabwe
3. Line should be drawn along the Zambezi River valley from the Indian Ocean to Mwenemutapa.

BLACKLINE MASTER 2

1. forming the mountains, filling the land with dust, the rain, the heavens, growing plants, mankind
2. sewing a cloth
3. in the sheltering rocks
4. Great Spirit, Piler up of rocks, Vessel overflowing with oil, Caller forth of the branching trees, Lord, Gracious One
5. *Possible answers:* The hymn singer acknowledges Mwari as a supreme creative force who made the earth and its people. The singer assumes a worshipful, dependent role in relation to Mwari.

CHAPTER TEST

A. 1. a; **2.** c; **3.** d; **4.** b; **5.** a

B. 6. Archaeologists have found expensive and rare items such as beads, cotton cloth, and Chinese porcelain in this inland settlement, which tell them that there was trade in this area.

7. The city was located between the copper and gold mines in the west and the coastal trading area. The city's government collected taxes on the metals before they were moved on to Sofala on the coast.

C. Answers will vary but should include that the Shona became wealthy through trade but that as other cultures began to come to the area to gain wealth for themselves, the Shona eventually lost much of their own wealth.

CHAPTER 13

BLACKLINE MASTER 1

1. wool, leather, salt, slaves, hides, wood, pitch, dyes, gold, pack animals; swords, spices, sugar, cotton goods, glass, crops
2. Southern Africa relied mostly on waterways, including rivers and oceans; Northern Africa relied more on overland routes.
3. Most of the cities are on or near water; their locations made them ideal trading posts.

BLACKLINE MASTER 2

1. Most likely they did not have adequate territory to grow grain, and perhaps the soil was not suited to crops.
2. They had built mosques.
3. Mombasa is the name of the island and the city on it.
4. *Possible answers* include impressed, awed, excited, and appreciative.

ANSWER KEY

CHAPTER TEST
A. 1. b; 2. b 3. d; 4. a; 5. c

B. It was a smooth, white building with high turrets that were visible from the sea. The building was up to three stories high with several staircases leading down to the sea.

C. Answers might include facts such as the following: It was an era of great trade with Arabia, Persia, and India, and Swahilis were part of a Muslim trade network that reached all the way to China. Cities like Kilwa were prosperous and powerful. People had adjusted to the marine environment and learned new skills, such as mining the reefs for coral to build homes with, and how to build ships for trading. There were neighborhood mosques for people to practice their religion and come together.

WRAP-UP TEST

1. Students' paragraphs should explain that Mecca began as the location of the Ka'ba, where idols and statues of the polytheistic peoples were kept, and then grew into the center of the Muslim faith. They should also mention that Muslims turn toward Mecca to pray and that one of the Five Pillars of Islam is for each Muslim to visit the city at least once in a lifetime.

2. Paragraphs should note that both groups were nomadic and lived off livestock and depended on camels. Both groups eventually converted to Islam and were known for their strength and ability to withstand the desert climate. The groups were different because of their location in the Islamic world, the Bedouin being from the Arabian Peninsula and the Berbers from North Africa. The groups dressed differently, the Bedouin in long robes and the Berbers mostly uncovered. The Bedouin accepted Arab rule, but the Berbers did not.

3. The spread of Islam began when the Prophet Muhammad began spreading God's messages to his friends and family and gradually converting the poor and slaves. After Muhammad's death, Abu Bakr continued to spread Islam throughout the Arabian Peninsula. Then Umar spread the boundaries of the Islamic rule to include the Sassanid Empire and part of the Byzantine Empire, as well as to northwest Africa and Spain.

4. Muslims believed that God spoke through Muhammad and told them to extend Islamic rule. They believed Islam was the only faith that promised to preserve human dignity and allow people to reach their potential. Muhammad said that, although war is hateful, it is sometimes necessary. Muslims believed that dying in a holy war ensured them a place in heaven.

5. The ulamas believed that God knew in advance if someone was going to sin and that the Quran was eternal. The Mutazilites believed Islamic religious teaching should fit the rules of logic and that humans have free will and control their ultimate destiny. They also believed that the Quran could not be eternal because only God is eternal

6. Students should note that many Muslim scholars made advances in the areas of philosophy and science that influenced the work of European philosophers and scientists hundreds of years later. They should mention the works of at least three people, which may include al-Haitham's work with light and the eye, ar-Razi's work with anatomy and diseases, al-Biruni's idea that the Earth rotates on an axis, Ibn Khaldun's beliefs about how societies change, and the writings of Ibn Tufayl and Ibn Rushd.

7. The ruler Mehmed organized an army of over 200,000 men as well as the Janissaries who were made up of the *devshirme* boys. These troops were equipped with guns as well as cannons that were casted from bronze or brass. The cannons easily broke through the walls of the city.

8. Students should describe how at least two of the African kings discussed in the book are treated by their subjects. for example, the Ghana of West Africa was kept on a raised platform above his subjects and his feet were not allowed to touch the ground. He was considered divine and no one could see him sleeping or eating. The sultan, Mansa Sulayman would sit upon a shaded platform surrounded by silk fabric and pillows. His subjects would be on the ground. The subjects of the Oba of Benin covered their faces and approached them from a low position, cowering, and would never turn their backs toward him. These treatments of the kings show that the king was held in very high esteem and the subjects were considered very lowly and inferior to the king.

9. Paragraphs should mention that the gold trade brought many traders to Africa, specifically Arab traders. These traders introduced the people of western Sudan to Islam. These people incorporated Islam into their traditional beliefs. The rulers of the people, the mansas, were mostly Muslims and encouraged the people to be more faithful to Islam.

10. Paragraphs should note that trade on the Swahili coast was prosperous because of its location near the Indian Ocean, making it an easy destination for traders from Arabia, the Persian Gulf, and western India. Swahili traders exchanged goods that they made or acquired locally or from their trade with people from areas farther inland.

ANSWERS FOR THE STUDENT STUDY GUIDE
CHAPTER 1

Word Bank
1. caravan 2. Ka'ba 3. trade 4. Bedouin 5. nomads

Word Play
shaykh; Check students' sentences.

Critical Thinking
1. g 2. d 3. b 4. a 5. c 6. e

Working with Primary Sources
1. He gave people shelter from their enemies and took care of them.
2. The poet's mood is sad, but loving and respectful of her brother's memory.
3. Until the day she dies and is buried.
4. She says she will remember him until she is dead. She also says she remembers him at the beginning and end of every day.

All Over the Map
1. Line should go from Mecca to Yemen, back to Mecca, and then diverge with one line to Egypt and Syria and one to Persia.
2. Persia: spices, perfumes, silk, cotton; Yemen – wheat, frankincense and myrrh for incense and perfumes, animal hides, ivory gold, textiles, and rhinoceros horn that comes in from Africa
3. trip from Mecca to Yemen to Mecca is about 2,400 miles; trip from Mecca to Yemen to Mecca and over to Persia is about 3,400 miles
4. Desert travel was dangerous because of the desert heat and the shortage of water. If caravans lost their way they could die from exhaustion and dehydration.
5. Traders made the journey and took the risk so they could prosper from trading goods with faraway places.

CHAPTER 2

Cast of Characters
Muhammad: the prophet of Islam
Abu Talib: uncle of the prophet Muhammad; raised him as a boy
Khadija: the first wife of the prophet Muhammad

Word Bank
1. convert 2. meditation, revelation 3. prophet, pilgrimage

Word Play
persecution; Check students' sentences.

With a Parent or Partner
2. verb; meditate 3. both noun and verb in current form 4. noun; reveal

Critical Thinking
1–4. Answers will vary.

Working with Primary Sources: Write About It
Essays should discuss how the rewards of shade, ample food and water, and comforts would appeal to people living in the harsh conditions of the desert.

Working with Primary Sources
1. Both passages talk about how being generous is a way of being dutiful to God; just as God looks after us, so we should care for the needy among us
2. look after people (such as orphans, beggars, and slaves) who have less
3. Answers will vary.

All Over the Map
Check students' maps for accuracy.
1. 500: Axum, fought between the king of Yemen and Christians; Yemeni king won. 570: Mecca, fought between people of Axum; Meccans withstood the attack. 624: Badr, fought between Muslims led by Muhammad as retaliation against Quraysh persecution of Muhammad and his followers; Muslims routed the Quraysh. 625: Uhud, Meccans won narrow victory over Muslims but withdrew. 627: Medina, Quraysh and Bedouin allies against Muslims in failed assault
2. People in Mecca and Medina lived according to traditional tribal rules and were threatened by the new society that Muhammad was setting up with his followers. Leaders persecuted the Muslims, who stood their ground and retaliated. In the end Muhammad's opponents were not strong enough to defeat him, and many converted to Islam.

ANSWER KEY

CHAPTER 3

Cast of Characters
Abu Bakr: Muhammad's best friend who became the Islamic leader after Muhammad's death in 632. He helped spread Islam throughout the Arabian Peninsula.
Umar: Muslim leader after Abu Bakr. He led the Islamic expansion across northern Africa.
Tariq: Berber general who led a Berber band across the Mediterranean Sea and into Spain in the name of Islam.

Word Bank
1. heir
2. deputy
3. resisters

Word Play
alliance; Check students' sentences.

Critical Thinking
3, 5, 1, 2, 4

Working with Primary Sources
1. powerful, formidable, brave, numerous, true
2. Arabs, Persians, Greeks, Romans
3. The first passage praises the Berbers and compares them to other admirable civilizations; the second passage describes details about Berber life.
4. He thinks highly of them.
5. Answers will vary.

All Over the Map
Arabian Peninsula: 632–634
Sassanid Empire: 634–651
Algeria and Morocco: 665–680
Spain: 711–716

CHAPTER 4

Cast of Characters
Umar: the second caliph of Islam, who was killed by a Christian slave
Uthman: the third caliph of Islam, who had God's messages to Muhammad collected, written, and then published as the Quran
Ali: leader of Islam after Uthman who was called "imam" rather than "caliph"; first Shiite leader.
Muawiyah: governor of Syria and cousin of Uthman who became Ali's successor
Hasan and **Husayn:** sons of Ali

Word Bank
1. *zakat* 2. administrator 3. factions 4. diplomacy 5. *jizya*

Critical Thinking
1. Uthman 2. Uthman, Ali 3. Uthman, Muawiyah 4. Ali 5. Muawiyah 6. Ali, Muawiyah 7. Uthman, Mawiyah 8. Ali 9. Ali 10. Muawiyah, Uthman

Working with Primary Sources
1. because they had agreed to a truce instead of letting God determine the outcome of the battle
2. under Ali's leadership
3. God's truth
4. they have a united purpose
5. Answers will vary.

Comprehension
1. to a cease-fire
2. They disagreed with Ali's action and had a meeting to discuss rebelling against him
3. They left Ali's camp and went on a rampage through southern Iraq.

All Over the Map
1. Check students' work against map on Student Edition page 49.
2. 640 miles
3. Red Sea, Persian Gulf, Indian Ocean, Arabian Sea, Mediterranean Sea, Black Sea, Caspian Sea, Aral Sea, Atlantic Ocean
4. as a means of trade and travel

CHAPTER 5

Cast of Characters
Ibn Battuta: Berber from Tangier, Morocco, who left an account of his 75,000-mile journey throughout the Islamic world
Abu Jafar al-Mansur: Abbasid caliph from 754 to 775, who supported Persian literature at his court and founded Baghdad
Fatima: daughter of Muhammad and wife of Ali

What Happened When?
662 — al Mansur founded the new capital at Baghdad, Iraq
749–750 — The Abbasids rode to victory against the Umayyad armies
874 — the 11th descendent of Ali died
969 — the Shi'i Dynasty, the Fatimids, set up another rival caliphate in Egypt
1258 — Baghdad was almost totally destroyed by the Mongol general Hulegu

Word Bank
1. descendants 2. provinces 3. geographic 4. lavish 5. radiating

Word Play
ornate

Critical Thinking
Fact: 4, 5, 7, 9, 10
Opinion: 1, 2, 3, 6, 8

Working with Primary Sources
1. Baghdad was a vast, prosperous, lavish city.
2. Check students' study guides.
3. The city was surrounded by desert but could support extensive gardens and plantings; animals and birds were imported from all over.
4. Check students' journals.

All Over the Map
1–3: check students' work against map on Student Edition page 55.
4. The city's location on the Tigris gave it access to the Persian Gulf and the other Islamic lands to the east, and its central location in Iraq on major trading routes gave it easy access to the western reaches in North Africa and the Mediterranean.
5. Check students' work.
6. Trace journey from Morocco along the coast of North Africa and the mediterranean to Egypt, then south along the eastern shore of the Red Sea to Mecca
7. By water or along the coast—by land would mean traveling by desert, which was both slow and dangerous
8. about 3,720 miles
9. a) 1,116 miles; b) 550 miles; c) 868 miles; d) 3,350 miles

CHAPTER 6

Cast of Characters
al-Ma'mun: caliph who tried to make the leading *ulama* swear that the Quran was not eternal
Ahmad ibn Hanbal: religious scholar who refused to take al-Ma'mun's oath
Abu Hamid Muhammad al-Ghazali: scholar who believed that Sufism brought people closer to God

Word Bank
1. piety 2. *ulama* 3. *tariqas* 4. hadiths 5. Mutazilites

Word Play
Sufis; Check students' sentences.

Critical Thinking
1. a 2. c 3. a, b

Working with Primary Sources
Ibn Battuta excerpt: check students' answers
Rubaiyat:
1. The roses of yesterday have faded and died.
2. The Persian kings will die because time is always passing. Just as roses grow and die, so do all people—even kings.
3. Pleasures: Book of verses, jug of wine, loaf of bread, a companion ("Thou," possibly God) singing
4. that life passes quickly, the way snow that falls on the desert quickly melts and disappears
5. Answers will vary.

ANSWER KEY

CHAPTER 7

Cast of Characters
Abu Jafar al-Ma'mun: Abbasid caliph who encouraged scholarly thinking and helped organize the House of Wisdom
Abu Ali Hasan Ibn al-Haitham: Muslim physicist and mathematician who studied light and its effect on the human eye
Abu Bakr Muhammad ar-Razi: Muslim physician who studied diseases and was the director of the Baghdad hospital
Abu Raihan al-Biruni: Muslim philosopher who precisely calculated the earth's radius
Abu Zayd ibn: North African scholar who developed a theory about changing societies
Ibn Rushd: Andalusian scholar who believed there is a connection between philosophy and religion; commented on the works of Aristotle
Ibn Tufayl: Andalusian writer who wrote *Alive, Son of Awake*
Abu Abdallah ibn Battuta: Moroccan geographer who traveled throughout Africa, the Middle East, and Asia and kept a detailed account of his travels
Omar Khayyám: Persian poet who wrote *The Rubaiyat*

Word Bank
1. theory 2. bequeathed 3. scriptures 4. observant 5. speculated
6. embarked, *rihla*

Word Play
imposed; Check students' sentences.

Critical Thinking
1. f 2. d 3. a 4. g 5. b 6. e

Working with Primary Sources
1. Three girls going to pick olives find the olive trees bare. They go to pick pears instead.
2. Answers will vary. A possibility: The girls will find the pear trees bare as well and proceed to another tree, and another, and another.
3. Answers will vary.
4. The repetition of names and key lines, as well as the repetitive, singsong structure, make the poem easy to memorize.

All Over the Map
2. Tangier along the northern coast of Africa through Algiers, Tunis, Tripoli, Alexandria, Cairo, to the Red Sea, then north to Jerusalem and then south on eastern side of Red Sea to Mecca.
3. Total distance of journey about 3,300 to 3,500 miles

CHAPTER 8

Cast of Characters
1. f 2. h 3. c 4. o 5. l 6. g 7. i 8. m 9. j 10. b 11. k 12. a 13. e 14. d

Word Bank
1. sovereignty 2. siege 3. vizier

Word Play
infidels; Check students' sentences.

What Happened When?
1071	Seljuk Turks defeated the Byzantines at the Battle of Manzikert
1258	Hulegu's Mongol hordes took Baghdad from the Seljuk Turks
1300	Mongols destroyed the Rum sultanate
1326	Osman's holdings now include all of northwestern Anatolia
1421–1451	Sultan Murad II introduced the *devshirme*
1451	Mehmed came to the throne
1453	The Ottomans took Constantinople
1516	Egypt added to the Ottoman province
1520	Suleyman came to the throne
1557	Suleymaniyya Mosque completed
1907	Revolutionaries forced Sultan Abdulhemid off the throne.
1922	Otoman Empire became the modern nation of Turkey

All Over the Map
1. Bursa 2. Cairo, Algiers, Tunis 3. Mediterranean Sea, Red Sea 4. about 1,200 miles

CHAPTER 9

Cast of Characters
Soninke: Bantu-speaking people of African grasslands
Berber: nomadic traders of the Sahara
Abdallah ibn Yasin, Muslim scholar who tried to convert the Berbers to Sunni Islam, first by teaching and then by force
Almoravids: group of Muslims who tried to reform Berber and West African religious observance, and who conquered most of North and West Africa

Word Bank
1. millet 2. dehydration 3. jihad 4. Ghana 5. *ribat* 6. grassland

Word Play
chiefdom; Check students' sentences.

Critical Thinking
1. f 2. i 3. a 4. j 5. g 6. k 7. h 8. b 9. e 10. c

Working with Primary Sources
1. in mosques
2. in domed buildings, groves, and thickets near the king's town
3. because Muslims were skilled in mathematics
4. Check students' books.
5. Sewn clothes signified privilege and prestige and set the king apart from other people.

All Over the Map
1-5. check against map on Student Edition page 116
6. draw route from Sahel to gold fields south of Kumbi Saleh
7. round trip distance about 3,000 miles
8. Rivers were useful for boat travel. It was easier to carry loads by boat, and there were no roads for overland trade.

CHAPTER 10

Cast of Characters
Sundiata: powerful chief of the Mande people who established the kingdom of Mali
Mansa Musa: king of Mali who was made famous by his many gifts of gold along his pilgrimage route to Mecca
Mansa Sulayman: king of Mali who, like Mansa Musa, upheld the Five Pillars of Islam and enforced Islamic law
Qasa: first wife of Sulayman
Banju: Sulayman's other wife who replaced Qasa
Sonni Ali: great ruler of the Songhay dynasty who captured Timbuktu in 1468
Muhammad Turé: a general under Sonni Ali who seized power of the Songhay dynasty after Ali's death

Word Bank
1. a) 2; b) 3; c) 4; d) 1
2. a) prosperity; b) dignitaries; c) alliance; d) prominent

Critical Thinking
2, 4, 5, 3, 1
7, 4, 1, 5, 3, 6, 2

Working with Primary Sources
al-Sadi quote
1. salt from Taghaza, gold from Bitu
2. They reap large profits and acquire fortunes.
3. People come to Timbuktu from every direction.

Working with Primary Sources
Photograph of market
1. Goods are being brought in and taken out by boat to the marketplace.
2. It was essential for trade and transportation.
3. Answers may vary. Possible difference: The goods being traded would have included gold, salt, iron, copper and salt. Possible similarity: The clothing would probably have looked similar.

All Over the Map
1. Buré and Bitu
2. Buré near headwaters of the Niger River; Bitu near the Volta River
3. Gao, Jenne, and Timbuktu
5. Locations on major rivers made them good places for boat trading on the river; they also had easy access to gold fields.
4. and 6. compare students' work with map on Student Edition page 116

ANSWER KEY

CHAPTER 11

Cast of Characters
Ewuare: Oba of Benin who came to power some time in the 1400s and engaged in successful wars of expansion
Oguola: Oba of Benin credited with bringing the art of bronze and brass casting to Benin

Word Bank
1. castings 2. lagoons 3. negotiate 4. precincts

Word Play
reverence; Check students' sentences.

Critical Thinking
1. c) and d) 2. b) and c) 3. b) and d)

Working with Primary Sources
1. Answers will vary
2. terracotta carving shows great skill and artistry; brass casting was a complicated process, so the artists were probably skilled craftsmen who would have been sponsored and supported by the ruling class
3. Because the ruling class doesn't grow its own food, farming would have to produce enough to feed it.
4. Archaeologists have discovered extraordinary artwork, indicating a class of artists and artisans.

All Over the Map
1, 2, 4. Check work against the map on student book page 130.
3. All the cities are either on or very close to the Niger River
5. Check answers for accuracy.
6. Traders could transport goods from the forests and grasslands up the Niger River to major trading centers such as Jenne and Gao. Heavy goods are more easily shipped by water.

CHAPTER 12

Cast of Characters
1. **Bantu**: people of southeastern Africa who spoke the Bantu language
2. **Shona**: descendants of the Bantu
3. **Mutota**: the last king of Great Zimbabwe
4. **Mutope**: Mutota's successor who extended the northern capital and opened trade with the coast

Word Bank
1. prestige 2. rift, sorghum 3. disdain 4. coincided 5. kraals

Word Play
kin; Check students' sentences.

Critical Thinking
1. d 2. h 3. j 4. i 5. a 6. c 7. g 8. e 9. f 10. b

Working with Primary Sources
1. Check students' work
2. The people need water so that the trees and plants can grow.
3. The Shona survived by planting millet and sorghum and also raising cattle. They would need water to cultivate their crops, and so grass could grow for their cattle to eat.
4. a bird called a fish eagle
5. The fish eagle migrated to their area every year during the rainy season, which was when the people most needed the rain god to send rain to their crops.
6. The Shona depended on farming and herding cattle for their survival, and the land where they lived was a dry and fragile environment. Therefore they needed an adequate supply of rain: to cultivate their crops and allow grass to grow for their herds. They believed rain came from the rain god Mwari, and that he could keep the rains away if he was displeased with them. So the hymn sings praises to Mwari so he will be pleased with the people and send them rain.

All Over the Map
1–2. Check all labeling against map on Student Edition page 142
3. Traders from the coastal cities of Kilwa and Sofala began traveling on the Zambezi River to trade with the Shona instead of using the old routes that passed through Great Zimbabwe. As a result, the ruling classes of Great Zimbabwe moved north along the Zambezi River in Mwenemutapa, so they could once again participate in the trade.
4. Shade the area between the Zambezi and Limpopo Rivers.
5. First near Mapungubwe; later in northern part of plateau near Mwenemutapa
6. Gold from Mwenemutapa through Great Zimbabwe to Sofala and Kilwa
7. Gold from Mwenemutapa, along Zambezi River through Shonaland; along coast to Kilwa and Sofala
8. Ships came from the south, in the Indian Ocean, and traveled up the Zambesi River (see map on Student Edition page 153)

CHAPTER 13

Cast of Characters
João de Barros: Portuguese writer and librarian who collected accounts of visits to African locations
Hasan bin Sulayman: 14th century king of Kilwa
Ibn Battuta: Berber from Tangier, Morocco, who left an account of his 75,000-mile journey throughout the Islamic world

Word Bank
1. migrated 2. dynasty 3. disembarked 4. quay 5. prestigious

Word Play
infidel; Check students' sentences.

Critical Thinking
3,1,6,2,5,4

Working with Primary Sources
1. As a trader, you could make a lot of money by having contact with merchants from all over. But you are dependent on neighboring cities for other kinds of food for your survival, so you are at risk if this trade was ever disrupted.
2. Two ways: he collected fees, or taxes, based on the goods merchants brought into the city. He was also entitled to half of the goods, which he could sell to other neighboring cities.
3. The city-states were not completely self-sufficient and had to rely on trade with their neighbors to get basic supplies of food, especially grains. They also needed to import goods from the mainland so they would have goods to exchange with the merchants who came from Asia and Arabia.

All Over the Map
1. Most exports from the Swahili were raw materials; most of the exports of Arabia, Persia, and India were manufactured materials.
2. Kilwa was the closest trading city to the gold fields of Zimbabwe
3. They must raise enough sheep and possibly other animals to sell the excels. Places that export wood and pitch must have lots of trees.
4. Some water routes are longer and some are shorter than land routes. However, shipping goods on water was easier and more direct than going through rough terrain or deserts on land.
5. Goods would have been transported by camels in caravans across the Sahara and through Asia.

www.ingramcontent.com/pod-product-compliance
Lightning Source LLC
LaVergne TN
LVHW080250260326
834688LV00042BA/1203